Five Oh

Fifty is the New F-Word
Book Five in the Val Fremden Mystery Series
Margaret Lashley

Copyright 2017 Margaret Lashley

More Praise for the Val Fremden Series

"Ms Lashley's writing style is brilliant and hilarious. The plot is imaginatively twisty, the situations are wacky, the characters are lovable, and there is a surprise ending that I never saw coming. I wish the author could write as fast as I can read!"

"I'm a man and these are "Chick" books, but I don't care, they're funny."

"Val and Pals enjoy another improbable romp with dwarfs, shyster lawyers, a cursed engagement ring and another zany adventure."

"Breathtakingly brilliant. I signed up for unlimited amazon reading just for these books. This last year has been rough and these books are a miracle."

"This series is warm, funny, well written and had me laughing ruefully the whole read."

"Of course, nothing goes as planned and hilarity ensues. Another nice romp by Margaret Lashley."

More Hilarious Val Fremden Mysteries

by Margaret Lashley
Absolute Zero
Glad One
Two Crazy
Three Dumb
What Four
Five Oh
Six Tricks
Seven Daze
Figure Eight
Cloud Nine

"Normal is way overrated."
Val Fremden

Chapter One

I thought I saw a dwarf sneaking out of Laverne's house last night. But I could have been wrong. It was dark. And I was hopped up on Nyquil.

Funny. Yesterday, I'd started the day feeling *lucky*. I'd survived my mother's "holiday hospitality" with most of my self-worth intact – and my boyfriend Tom and I'd made the journey home without a hitch.

Well, that wasn't quite true. There had been *two* hitches. But compared to the family fruitcake disaster I'd just lived through, they'd weighed in as pretty minor. After all, they were just a close brush with death and a marriage proposal.

YESTERDAY, DURING THE ride home from Greenville, redneck capital of...*the world*, a rotten virus had walloped me in the head like a Rock'Em Sock'Em Robot. It was the second sucker-punch to knock me for a loop that day. The first had been when my boyfriend Tom surprised me with an engagement ring. After spewing a mouthful of RC Cola all over the dash of his truck like a sprinkler-head gone haywire, my mind had seized up with an all-too-familiar uncertainty. For the life of me, when it came to the idea of matrimony, I couldn't decide whether to laugh for joy or scream with terror.

I knew marrying Tom was *my* choice, but I wasn't ready to make it. Not yet. All I'd known for certain at that moment was that I hadn't wanted to disappoint Tom. So I'd smiled, swallowed my fears, and played along with the engagement – then tried my best not to crap my pants before we got back home to St. Pete Beach.

During the five-hour drive, I'd felt increasingly weak and wobbly. By the time we reached Lake City, the anxiety that clouded my mind had grown so thick and heavy I could barely hold my head up. Somewhere around Ocala, my throat began to burn like fire. Hot pressure built up in my nose. Beads of sweat burst out above my lip.

That's when I knew for sure I hadn't been swept off my feet by love. I'd been done in by the flu.

I'd never been a good patient. Yesterday had proved that point again in spades. A tsunami of grouchiness had overtaken me. By the time poor Tom finally got me home, I'd been crabby enough to destroy Tokyo. He'd dropped me and my suitcase at the front door and fled. A veritable drive-by, dump-off. Who could blame him?

In all fairness to Tom, I'd begged him to leave me to wallow in my own wretchedness last night. There was no point in him getting sick, too. And I sure as heck didn't need him around to witness my hideous transformation into the red-eyed monster from planet Phlegm.

So, I'd stumbled into my house alone last night and collapsed onto my bed. I was beyond miserable. And, of course, I couldn't sleep. Around 2 a.m., I'd been in the bathroom slugging back my fourth shot of Nyquil when I'd heard a strange sound. With nothing else pressing on my agenda at that moment, I'd squandered what was left of my energy and dragged myself into the living room and peeked between the slats in the blinds.

That's when I thought I saw the dwarf sneaking down Laverne's driveway. But like I said, it was dark. And it could have been the Nyquil. The last time I'd taken the stuff I'd mistaken the mailman for Elvis.

A LIGHT TAPPING AT my front door woke me from a shallow, fitful sleep. I cracked open a crusty eye. My retina was instantly seared by the laser-white light radiating around the edges of the bedroom blinds like a million-megawatt picture frame. I squeezed my eye shut and groaned.

"*Ughh...*"

The tapping came again. Louder and more persistent this time. Absolutely no part of my body whatsoever wanted to move. But, as usual, I was overridden by ingrained Southern guilt. *I couldn't not answer the door, for heaven's sake!*

"Dang it!" I threw back the covers and drug myself out of bed. I wrapped my freezing body in my ratty bathrobe and fumbled down the hallway. One blurry, bloodshot eye strained to focus through the front-door peephole. A tall, thin, old lady with strawberry blond curls and a donkey face came into view. She stood at the door grinning like a chimp with a banana-split hangover. It was my next-door neighbor, Laverne Cowens. I sighed and opened the door.

"Hey, Laverne," I rasped. "Just so you know, I could be highly contagious."

"Highly who? I thought you were my neighbor, Val Fremden," Laverne joked.

"Huh," I grunted. Through my stuffy nose, it sounded more like "honk."

The twinkle in her bulgy eyes faded a notch as she studied my face. A sympathetic pout formed on her lips. "Awe, honey. I was just trying to be funny. You look awful!"

"Thanks." I blew what was left of my brains into a sodden tissue.

"You crawl back into bed. I'll make you some chicken soup."

"You don't have to –"

"Nonsense!" Laverne clomped inside on her gold high heels. She shooed me toward my bedroom with a thin, liver-spotted hand. "Just tell me one thing first, honey. Where's your can opener?"

The right side of my mouth curled upward. I flailed a weak arm in the direction of the kitchen. "Third drawer to the left."

"All righty, then. Scoot!"

I shuffled my way down the hall toward the bathroom as Laverne banged my pots and pans around like a naughty two-year-old. I avoided my reflection in the vanity mirror. I felt sick enough already.

In my addle-brained state, I thought if I could brush my matted hair, I'd feel better. I picked up the brush and forced it into my hair. It stuck in place like it was covered in Crazy Glue. *Great.* I yanked the brush out of the rat's nest encircling my head and fumbled my way back to bed.

As I lay there pondering the idea that death might be a pleasant option, that crazy old lady who lives next door managed to make me laugh. From the kitchen, Laverne, bubble-headed sage and former Vegas showgirl, was belting out a horrendously off-key rendition of *Zippity Do Da*, punctuating it randomly with an occasional, "Gosh, dang it!"

I sighed and relaxed into the bed covers as my fevered mind envisioned Laverne doing the can-can with a can of soup in each hand.

I was lying on an operating table. A masked doctor held my detached heart up to the light.

"What's your opinion?" the doctor asked the man next to him, a clown wearing a brown derby hat with a daisy sticking out of it.

"Lederhosen," the clown said.

"Just as I suspected," the masked surgeon said. "Get her out of here."

An orderly appeared from the mist, looking suspiciously like Sasquatch in blue scrubs. He grabbed my foot and started yanking it....

I woke with a start. Laverne was standing at the foot of my bed, shaking my left foot through the bedspread.

"Hey, honey. Wake up. Soup's on." She held my big blue mixing bowl in her hands. "Eat up. Then I want to hear all about your trip to your mom's."

Laverne watched me patiently, grinning in her mother donkey sort of way, as I hauled my body to sitting and settled myself in amongst the bed pillows.

"Where do I start?" I groaned.

"Why, at the beginning, of course." She stretched her long, spidery arms across the bed to hand me the bowl of soup. As I reached for it, she stopped midway, leaving my fingers grasping feebly at the air like a toddler begging to be picked up.

"Where'd you get that?" she asked.

"Get what?"

"That ring."

"Oh." I winced weakly. "Tom gave it to me. I guess...we're...*engaged*, sort of."

Laverne eyed the ring dubiously. "It doesn't *look* like an engagement ring."

"I know. It's a blue sapphire. Tom said it was unusual, because *I'm* so unusual."

"Huh. Let me see it."

I held my hand out.

"No," Laverne said. "I mean take it off. Let me *see* it."

I did as I was told. Laverne set the bowl of soup on the nightstand, grabbed the ring and held it up to the ceiling light. One bulgy eye squinted as the other opened wide to study the inside the band. "It's engraved," she needlessly informed me. "I Luv U. *Aww.* L-U-V." She looked over and shot me a full-denture grin. "How sweet!"

"Yeah. Don't remind me," I said grumpily. "It's pretty sappy. And the dumb spelling doesn't help, either. But I've decided to chalk it up to lack of space, rather than Tom's lack of taste."

Laverne's smiling face wilted like a plucked daisy in the sun. "Tom's a good guy, you know."

I sighed. "I know. I'm sorry. I'm just not feeling the greatest right now."

"Sure. That's it," Laverne said, and perked back up. "Eat your soup. It'll help."

I leaned across the pillows and reached sideways for the soup. As I did, my elbow hit the bowl and knocked it halfway off the nightstand. Laverne and I gasped and watched in slow-motion horror as the soup teetered precariously on the edge of the table.

"I got it," I cried, and tried to grab the bowl from the bottom. But I overreacted and swatted the bowl upward instead. It did a back flip, bounced off the nightstand and hit the rug with a wet thud. A quart of chicken-noodle soup splattered all over the place.

"Oh, crap," I groaned, and sank back into the pillows.

"My lordy!" Laverne said. She crinkled her nose at the mess and handed me back my engagement ring. I groaned, slipped it on my finger, then tried to get out of bed.

"What are you doing?" Laverne demanded.

"Gotta...clean up...this mess," I mumbled.

"Nothin' doin! It wasn't your fault, honey. No use crying over spilled soup. I'll fetch you another bowl and then clean this up myself."

"But..."

"No buts! It's not so bad, sugar. And you need to rest." Laverne studied me for a moment, then winked. "And if you finish your soup, young lady, you can have a piece of cherry pie."

My heart lurched in my congested chest. Laverne's cooking skills were legendary – in the way Jack the Ripper was legendary for making house calls.

"Did *you* make the pie?" I asked.

"Sure did!" Laverne beamed. "In my new cooking class. *Southern Classic Desserts.*"

My life flashed before my eyes. *Think of something, quick!* "Uh...thanks, Laverne. It sounds delicious. Really. But I have to pass. I have a wedding dress to fit into, remember?"

Laverne crinkled her nose, then brightened like a three-watt bulb. "Oh, that's right! I didn't think about that, sugar." She grinned and pointed an index finger toward the ceiling. "One new soup, coming up!" She spun on her high heels and bounced out the bedroom door.

I melted back into the pillows. Relief washed over me like a warm, Gulf tide. I'd narrowly evaded Laverne's cooking, and, so far, Tom's insistence on getting married. The dress I had to fit into wasn't for *my* wedding. It was for my best friend Milly's. She and Vance would be tying the knot in four months. I blew my swollen clown nose and sighed.

Better you than me, girlfriend. Better you than me.

Chapter Two

It was some kind of new record for me. January, February and March had gone by without a single calamity or catastrophe to speak of. Work at Griffith & Maas was good – I'd even gotten a raise. I still had all my fingers and toes, and I'd lost three pounds. All in all, it had been a banner start to the new year.

Even the bittersweet aftertaste of mom's Christmas fruitcake had finally faded. Partially because it had been replaced by a new sourness on the tip of my tongue. It was also the fault of a cake. But this time, it was a *birthday* cake. *Mine.* Tomorrow I would, unofficially, turn fifty.

Of course, that milestone had already *officially* occurred back on December 22. But if there was one good thing about being found by the side of the road as a baby, it was this; I could still unofficially claim the later birth date on my bogus birth certificate.

When she'd taken me in, my adoptive mom and fruitcake saboteur, Lucille Jolly, had chosen April Fools' Day as my birth date because she'd thought it was funny. But this year in particular, it had been kind of a lifesaver. By claiming April 1 as my birthday, I'd been able to, *at least in my own mind*, delay my inevitable demise for another 68 days. It would have been *69* days if this had been a leap year. But, as my luck would have it, it hadn't been.

The big five-oh. Oh boy....

To top it off, today was Friday. That meant I had to spend my last day in my forties at work. *Crap on a cracker.* It's not that I hated my job, per se. It was just...well, work wasn't a four-letter word for nothing.

"HOW'S IT FEEL TO BE officially old?" my best friend and boss Milly Halbert joked as I drug myself begrudgingly through the door at the accounting firm of Griffith and Maas.

"Ha ha. Real funny. How's it feel to be officially doomed?"

The smarmy smile evaporated from Milly's impish face. "What do you mean?"

"Your impending nuptials. I may be old, Milly, but at least I'm still *free.* Besides, you're only like, two years younger than me."

"Two and a *half.*" Milly twirled a lock of blonde hair around her finger. "And what's so bad about being married?"

"I guess you'll find out soon enough."

Milly scowled and bit a fingernail. "Look, just because it didn't work out for *you* doesn't mean –"

"Sorry. You're right, Milly." I was in no mood to think about marriage *or* to rain on Milly's wedding parade. *Turning fifty is a pity party for one. I shouldn't invite others along for the ride.*

"Listen," I said. "Let's start over." I turned my back to Milly, then spun back around. "Good morning, Milly!" I said cheerily, and shot her a smile worthy of a toothpaste commercial.

Milly eyed me with suspicion. "Good morning, Val."

"Nice weather we're having."

"What are you talking about?"

"It's sunny with a high of 76 degrees today," I said with an air of empty-headed innocence.

Milly scowled. "Val, don't be weird."

"Talking about the weather is *weird?*"

"No. *Being normal.* For *you*...well...it's just *weird.*"

I slumped as my lips twisted with sarcasm. "Gee. Thanks."

"You know what I mean."

The *really* weird thing was, *I did*. "Huh. I figured that, you know, now that I'm officially *old*, I'd turn over a new leaf."

Milly frowned. "I liked the *old* leaf."

I sneered. "So what? Now, even my *leaf* is old?"

Milly laughed, causing her button nose to crinkle. "You're a nut. You know that, don't you?"

I grinned through one side of my mouth. "So are you. Now that we've established that, how are the wedding plans going?"

Milly's big, green eyes went a bit googly. "Pretty good, actually. We've got everything nailed down except the honeymoon."

"Nailed down, huh?" I sneered. "Well, if that isn't the perfect term for matrimony, I don't know what is."

Milly shook her head and grinned. "Incorrigible. Now *there's* the old Val I know and love."

"Do me a favor. Don't say 'old' and 'Val' in the same sentence. Remember, it'll be *your* turn soon enough."

"Yes ma'am."

I shot Milly a dirty look.

"Ooops," Milly teased. "Did I say ma'am? Well, excuse me! What I meant to say was, 'Can I take you to lunch today for your birthday, *hot stuff?*'"

I grinned. "Now *that's* more like it. But nope. Sorry. Tom's already beat you to it. But you're coming to the party tomorrow night, right?"

"Natch!" Milly winked, then wrinkled her brow like a boss. "Now, Ms. Valiant Fremden, I suggest you get to work."

"Yes *ma'am,* Ms. Millicent Halbert."

IF I HAD TO PICK A place to spend my last moments of being forty, a sushi lunch at Ming Ming's with Tom wasn't a bad call. I sat at a small table by the plate glass window and waited for my buff, blond cop, Lieutenant Thomas Foreman, to make his appearance.

Then I waited some more.

I checked my phone. I studied the menu. I drummed my nails on the table. I drank a whole glass of ginger tea. Still, no Tom. According to the clock on the wall, he was fifteen minutes late. That wasn't like him. Finally, I waived the waiter over and ordered.

My finger was on the 'send' button of a less-than-cordial text to Tom when I looked up and saw his silver 4Runner pull into the parking lot. He jumped out and sprinted to the door, his face one big, handsome apology.

"I'm sorry I'm late!" he called across the tiny restaurant.

My lips twisted in doubt. He kissed them anyway.

"What was the hold up?" I asked.

"I'm helping Jorge study for his exams," he said, pulling out a chair.

"I know. But we had a date." *It's my last day in my forties, for crying out loud!*

Tom sat down and studied my face. "Val, Jorge's a complete nervous wreck."

I frowned. "I guess that tops being a complete *drunken* wreck."

The hurt and disappointment on Tom's face made my cheeks flush with heat.

"Sorry, Tom. Really. I mean...I think it's great Jorge wants to get his job back on the police force. It's just...well, lately, he's been taking a lot more of *our time* than I thought he would."

To my relief, Tom smiled and reached across the table to take my hand. "I know," he said. "And I'm sorry. I'll make it up to you. I promise. Did you order for me?"

"No. I wasn't sure you were coming."

Tom's sea-green eyes lost their sparkle. "Really? After two years together, you still have no confidence in me, do you?"

"It's not that."

"Then what?"

I shrugged. "I don't know. Maybe I didn't know what you wanted to *eat* today, okay?"

"I always get the same thing."

"Sure. But the first time I assume that and go ahead and order for you, then you're *stuck* with it. I mean...you know, you're out of options. Your fate is sealed."

Tom stared at me blankly.

I tried to backtrack. "It's like that old saying, you know? That whole 'ass outta you and me' thing."

Tom let go of my hand. "Are you feeling trapped, Val?"

My face went fifty degrees hotter. "No."

Tom studied me a moment more. I tried not to break under his scrutiny, but I couldn't help myself.

"Honestly, it's not that," I said. "I guess I'm just...geeze, Tom! *Today is my last day of being in my forties!*"

Tom's serious stare evaporated into a grin. "Oh. *That's* what this is all about."

I managed an apologetic smile. "Sorry for making this all about me." I sighed and asked, "How's it going with Jorge, anyway?"

Tom relaxed and shifted back in his seat. He seemed relieved the conversation was back in familiar territory. "Okay, I suppose. But with his PTSD, Jorge won't be able to handle a regular beat. I think he's better suited to an office job now. Clerical stuff. You know, background support for cops on the street. Stuff like that."

"Oh. I'm glad to hear that. I was worried about him having to deal with criminals. He's such a...I dunno...*soft touch*."

Tom took my hand again and squeezed it. "Yeah. Too bad you never knew him before his family got killed in that accident. He was a different guy. I guess his confidence will never be back on par with what it was. But hey, enough about Jorge. How's my birthday gal doing?"

I sighed. "Feeling pretty old, actually."

"Awe, fifty isn't so bad, Val. Now, fifty-five? *That's* the killer."

"Why?"

"That's when you're on the back-slide to sixty. Thankfully, it's still a long slide away for both of us."

I rolled my eyes and sneered. "That makes me feel *sooo* much better."

Tom laughed. "Hey, you'll always be younger than *me*."

The thought cheered me up a little, even though Tom had less than a year on me. "True enough, old man," I joked. "So, when are Jorge's exams again?"

"On Monday. Goober and Winky are going with him for moral support."

"You're not going?"

"No. I've got other plans."

"What plans?"

Tom shot me his infamous boyish grin. "I guess you'll have to wait until tomorrow to find out."

I scowled. "You know I'm lousy at waiting."

"Yeah." Tom winked. "That's why it's so much fun to tell you now."

I pouted and punched Tom on the arm. "Just for that, you can't have any of my sea creature roll."

Tom flinched in mock pain. "Ouch. Thanks a lot, Miss Meanie." His playful eyes suddenly switched to seduction mode. "I guess I can live with that – as long as I can have a roll with you later tonight?"

I stuck my nose in the air and looked at the ceiling to my left. "I guess you'll have to wait until tonight to find out."

Tom snickered. "Double ouch."

THAT EVENING, TOM CAME over and helped me set up for the party. Without any needling from me, he got to work and wiped down the lawn furniture, spruced up the tiki hut, and stacked logs in the fire pit he'd built for me. I shook my head in disbelief. A year had already flown by since he'd surprised me on my last birthday. He'd not only built the fire pit – he'd arranged a complete backyard makeover while I was at a spa with Milly. *He really is quite the guy....*

As I made potato salad and prepped for the party, the occasional glimpse of Tom working out in the backyard caused a dull, melancholy throbbing in my heart. Domestic happiness always looked so good on paper...but reality had proven time and again to be so different than what I'd envisioned in my dreams. As a friend of mine used to say, "Nice from afar, but far from nice."

"Think you got enough pepper in there?" Tom's warm, deep voice sounded behind me, startling me out of my daydream.

"Huh?" I asked as he slipped his strong hands around my waist. I looked down at a bowl of marinade I'd been preparing. I'd absently ground a small mountain of peppercorns into it. "Oh. Crap." I set the peppermill on the kitchen counter and stared down at the hill of black crumbles floating atop the puddle of Italian salad dressing.

"What were you thinking about?" Tom asked, and gently twirled me around to face him.

"Uh...just the idea of turning the big five-oh," I lied.

Tom smiled and kissed me. "I know how you hate waiting. How about I give you an early birthday present?" He rubbed his cheek against mine, then nibbled my earlobe.

"What did...you...have in mind?" I stuttered, as my back arched involuntarily. Neck nuzzling was my Kryptonite, and Tom darn well knew it.

"I was thinking of something fitting for the occasion," he whispered, then lightly bit my earlobe again. "How about five 'O's' in a row?"

Geeze. How could a girl argue with that?

Chapter Three

"Where's your birthday cake?" tall, lanky Goober asked as he bent over and scrounged a beer from my fridge. I was in the kitchen spearing steaks with a long serving fork. I lifted a slab of meat from the peppery marinade and laid it on a platter. Winky watched dreamily from his perch on a stool at the counter, drooling like a ginger-haired hound dog.

"I bet the dang fire department done confiscated it," Winky squawked at Goober, his eyes never leaving the steaks. "Fire hazard with all them candles, you know." The freckle-faced redneck looked up at me. "What you up to now, Val? Fifty thousand?" He winked, then laughed at his own joke like a deranged woodpecker.

"Ha ha," I said.

"So where is it?" Goober asked, and popped the top on a can of Fosters.

"Uh...what?" I asked.

"The cake," Goober said. He took a long slug of beer.

I bit my lip and muttered, "Laverne hasn't brought it over yet."

Both guys froze in place, mouths full of beer, like those wooly mammoths found in the arctic ice with green grass in their maws. They swallowed hard, then their jaws fell open like a pair of busted tailgates.

"Oh no," Goober said. He shook his bald head and blew out a low whistle. "Come on, now, Val. Don't tell me *Laverne's* making your cake?"

I flinched and turned my face away. "I'm afraid so...."

"Gaul dang it!" Winky spat. "I was lookin' forward to havin' me some birthday cake!"

"I know, I know!" I said. "But what could I say? She's taking this class at the senior citizens center and I just couldn't –"

"Pull yourself together, Val!" Goober barked. "Winky, you too." He spoke like a drill sergeant trying to keep his troops from losing it under enemy fire. "Listen up! If we're gonna survive this, we need a plan."

The three of us formed a loose huddle with our commanding officer, Sergeant Peanut Head. "Someone's got to sneak in next door and apprehend that cake before lamebrain Laverne does us all in again with another round of WMDs."

"WMDs?" Winky asked.

"Weapons of mass diarrhea," Goober said. Winky nodded solemnly.

"Look, Goober. We can't," I argued. "If we go sneaking into her house like a SWAT team, we might give her a heart attack. She's an old lady."

Goober snickered. "You should know."

"What?" I said, and whacked him with a dishtowel.

"Stop it, you two!" Winky whined. "We got to do something!" He rubbed his substantial beer belly. "My gut's startin' to boil just thinkin' 'bout her Thanksgivin' crapperoni casserole."

"Right," Goober said. He glanced around the room, then smoothed his bushy moustache with a thumb and forefinger. "If abscondination is off the table, we're left with only one viable option."

"Abscondination?" I asked Goober.

"This is not the time to be questioning my authority to employ poetic license, Val."

Desperation wracked Winky's face. "I don't care what kind a scondinaiton stuff you use, as long as that gaul-dang killer cake stays off the table, too."

"So what's our other option?" I asked, not at all sure I wanted to know.

"An unfortunate accident," Goober said matter-of-factly.

The left side of my mouth jerked up like it was caught on a fishhook. "You're talking about the *cake*, right?"

Goober's bushy eyebrows met in the middle of his forehead. "Of course! We're not *animals*, Val!"

Winky shamed me with pursed lips and a head wag.

"Okay," I caved. "All right. I'm in. But I don't want to know the details."

"Mum's the word," Goober said. Winky nodded and put a pudgy finger to his lips.

As if on cue, the front doorbell rang. I opened it to find Laverne standing there holding what could have possibly been mistaken for a cake – if I'd recently taken a large swig of Nyquil.

"Hiya, birthday girl!" Laverne beamed. "Surprise!"

Against my will, my leery eyes returned to the cake. Nope. Nyquil had nothing to do with this fiasco. Laverne's culinary catastrophe on a platter was roundish and lumpy – about the size and shape of a half-deflated volleyball drop-kicked from an airplane. It was smeared in what I hoped with every fiber of my being was chocolate icing. Piped onto it in a melty, urine-colored substance were the words, Happy Birtday Val. I would have mentioned the missing H to Laverne, but given how wrong the rest of the cake was, it didn't really seem to matter.

"Wow!" I said, and smiled up at Laverne. "You really outdid yourself with this one! Here, let me take it."

My fingers wrapped around the cake plate and I tugged it out of Laverne's hands. As I turned toward the right, I caught a glimpse of something red and splotchy in the corner of my eye. Before my brain could make the connection, Winky ran me over like a Black Friday bargain hunter. I stumbled, head first, into the wall. Knocked senseless, I took a fumbling step backward, tripped on the living room rug and landed flat on my butt in the middle of the living room floor. Against all odds, I still had a-grip on the platter. As my butt hit the floor, the cake, which apparently went airborne, flopped back onto the platter in my lap with a squishy thud.

"Oh my lord!" Laverne cried out. "Are you alright, sugar?"

"I...think so." I looked down. The cake leered back at me between a swirl of white stars. Like a nuclear-war-proof cockroach, the hideous thing had survived intact. I, on the other hand, had a knot on my forehead the size of a half a lemon.

"Sorry. I musta tripped," Winky said. "Let me help you up." He held out a pudgy hand and stared me in the eye. Even his freckles looked disappointed. He whispered from the side of his mouth, "It's time for Plan B."

"Get away from me," I snapped. I set the cake on the floor, hauled myself to standing and hoisted up the chocolate-covered monstrosity. Fuming, I marched toward the kitchen, Laverne on my heels. As I rounded the countertop bar, a dark object shot out from under the cabinets and darted across the floor. My mind turned to mush.

"Aaaarrhhhggg!" I shrieked.

Laverne's birthday cake flew up and out of my hands as if someone had mashed my ejector button.

"Rat! Rat!" I screamed and made a frantic dash for the back door, nearly mowing poor Laverne down in my path. If she hadn't grabbed a hold of my arm for support, I probably would have knocked her off her feet like a bowling pin.

"What's wrong, sugar?" Laverne asked, clutching at me as if I was the last life boat on the Titanic.

"Where's Tom?" I cried out, wild-eyed. "There's a rat in the kitchen!"

"Oh my word!" Laverne said. "Is that all? I'll go get him. Now you go sit on the couch and calm down."

"I...uh.... Oh no! Your cake, Laverne!"

"It's okay, sugar. Look," she let go of my arm and pointed toward the kitchen counter.

Still in shock, I turned back toward the kitchen and could scarcely believe my eyes. The dark, hulking glob of a cake had crash-landed, right-side-up, on the counter, none the worse for wear. Like all the hideous buildings constructed in the 1960's, that dang thing was indestructible. As stumbled over to it and stared at it in disbelief, Goober and Winky walked up and stood on either side of me.

"Unbelievable," Goober said. "Dang thing looks like an asteroid."

"It looks like it came from someone's nether regions, all right," Winky sneered.

"Look," I said, my back squirming at the thought of a rodent in my kitchen. "We've got bigger problems. I can't do anything until we find that rat!"

Goober nudged shoulders with me. "Look here." He fished around inside his sport jacket and pulled out a rubber rat tied to a ball of string.

"What?" I shrieked and nearly fell over. "Are you kidding me? Why did you...I mean...What the hell were you doing with that thing in your jacket, anyway?"

Goober shrugged. "Hey. It comes in handy more than you'd think."

"Great going, Val," Winky said. He looked as if he'd been stewed in country gravy. "You done blowed two perfectly good tactical ops to H-E-double-toothpicks."

"What are you talking about?"

"You said you wanted to remain unapprised of tactical details," Goober said.

"Okay. That's true," I said angrily. "But do all of your plans have to involve my imminent demise?"

The guys shrugged. "Desperate times call for desperate measurements," Winky said.

"Thanks for letting me know where I stand," I said. "Geeze! Just look at that thing. I don't think a stick of *dynamite* could get rid of it."

The three of us stared at the chocolate-smeared nemesis of impeding gastric doom.

"I don't think my colon can survive a slice of that," Winky whined.

"We'll have to think of something else," Goober said. "Shhh. Laverne's coming back."

Laverne ambled through the back sliding glass door and smiled. "Look at you three! Can't take your eyes off my cake. Well, mitts off! You'll have to wait 'til after dinner for a piece!"

We smiled sheepishly at Laverne. Tom appeared behind her with a hammer in his hand.

"Where's the rat?" Tom asked.

"It was a joke," Goober said, and pulled the rubber rat out of his jacket pocket.

Tom shot us a grin. "You guys and your birthday pranks. And that cake...oh my lord! You really got Val good with that one!"

Winky and Goober forced smiles. I glanced over at Laverne. She was beaming proudly, oblivious to Tom's remarks. I loved that about her.

Tom put his arm around my waist and kissed me. "Looks like you're none the worse for wear. Hey. Where's your ring?"

I looked down at my hand. "Oh. I took it off while I was prepping the steaks."

Tom's smile faded slightly. "Oh."

"For safekeeping," I explained. "It's in the ceramic ring holder on the windowsill."

I walked over to the sink and picked up the ring. "See? Here it is." As I turned back around to face Tom, my hand hit the neck of the faucet. I felt the ring jump from between my fingers. A small, dull, tinny sound echoed in my ears as it hit the stainless steel sink. Time slowed to a snail's pace as I turned and watched my engagement ring bounce once, then drop into the open maw of the garbage disposal.

"Oh no!" I said. "It's gone down the disposal!"

"You've got to be kidding," Tom said. "Please say it's another prank."

I shook my head. "Not this time. I'm sorry!"

Tom ran over to the sink. "What can we do to get it out?"

"Well, now, there's no need to panic," Laverne said cheerily. "We've got our resident mechanical genius in the house tonight."

Everyone turned to Winky.

"Don't look at me!" he said, his face twisted with disgust. "I ain't stickin' my hand down there. It's too gaul-dang scary."

"Good grief. Let me have a look," Goober said. He grabbed my steak fork and walked over and poked around at the sink for a moment as we all stood around and stared. "I can't see anything. Need more light." Goober looked around and reached a long, lanky arm toward a switch on the wall. My eyes bugged out like a cartoon character.

"Stop!" I screeched, and took a flying leap at Goober.

Like a bullfighter in the ring, Goober stepped back and narrowly escaped my clumsy side-tackle. My shoulder barely grazed him as I flew by. Having missed my target, momentum forced me to find a new one. I slammed into the kitchen cabinets and surfed halfway across the counter until something stopped my headlong slide. It was Laverne's birthday cake. I ricocheted off it like a billiard ball, knocking it onto the floor.

A cacophony of yelps and profanity filled my tiny kitchen.

"What in the world is going on?" Goober yelled.

"Are you all right?" Tom asked anxiously. He and Goober helped me off the counter.

"Goober...that switch," I gasped, trying to catch my breath. "It was for the garbage disposal."

"Oh," Goober said. Then comprehension caused the whites of his eyes to double. "Geeze! Good thing –"

"Oh my poor cake!" Laverne cried out.

Our heads turned in unison like a basket of kittens watching a toy. Laverne's hideous confection lay splattered in a lumpy pile on the floor like the mangled remains of the creature from the black lagoon bakery. The third time had, indeed, been the charm.

Goober leaned over and whispered in my ear, "Nice work."

"Somebody put some duck tape on that switch," Winky said. "I'll have a look see at that dang dispose-it-all in the mornin'. Now somebody call Milly. See if she can pick us up a new cake on her way here."

We all stared at Winky. We weren't used to him barking orders.

"What?" he asked. "I done told y'all. I want me some dad-burned birthday cake!"

Chapter Four

"What's with the duct tape?" Milly said as she set the replacement birthday cake on the kitchen counter next to the sink.

"Long story," I said. "You see...hey! Why are there Smurfs on my cake?"

Milly shrugged. "It was either that or cowboys and Indians. Last minute beggars can't be choosers, you know."

"Fair enough. Thanks."

"Natch'. So, what happened to Laverne's cake?"

"Unfortunate accident. It's resting peacefully in the garbage can in the backyard."

"My congratulations...I mean, condolences."

Milly shot me a wink and a smile, and I wrapped my arms around her. "Thanks for saving the day, Mil. Could you do me one more favor?"

"What?"

"Go tell Laverne how disappointed you are at not being able to try her cake. She's pretty bummed about the whole thing."

"Sure. That's what best friends are for, right? We lie to cover each other's backsides."

I grinned. "Exactly. And given the size of our backsides, we should be best friends forever."

Milly smirked and headed off to find Laverne. I stared down at six blue Smurfs grinning manically and dancing around a red toadstool dotted with white stars.

Well, at least they spelled "birthday" right.

"OH, YOU SHOULDN'T HAVE, Laverne!" I said and held up a shiny, gold, thong bikini.

Laverne grinned and relaxed into the couch cushions. Two gin cocktails had softened the blow of her cake's spectacular demise. "I think it'll come in handy soon," she said with an air of mystery. Tom, who was sitting next to her, nudged the old woman on the shoulder and laughed.

I dropped the bikini back into the gift bag and reached for a yellow envelope wedged between two other gifts laid out on the coffee table in front of me. "From Milly and Vance," I read aloud. I looked up at the two love birds. Milly was nestled like a kitten in Vance's lap in my easy chair.

"To my best friend," Milly said and raised a glass of white wine. Vance pouted at her words and pulled her closer. Milly giggled and kissed him.

The sight sent a twinge through my heart. My 'best friends forever' plan with Milly could face some tough competition in the months ahead. I opened the envelope and pulled out a hand-written note. "Good for one massage at Massage-O-Matic." I forced a grin at the lovey-dovey pair. "Thanks, you two!"

"I called and made a reservation for you, Val," Milly smirked. "Given your unfortunate history with coupons, I figured it was best." Vance laughed knowingly, and I suddenly realized he had become her confidant. That strange twinge shot through my heart again. *I thought I'd sworn Milly to secrecy over that incident at the spa where a hot masseuse had pulled a coupon for hemorrhoid cream from the back of my naked thigh....*

"That sounds like a story worth hearing," Tom said, interrupting my thoughts. I realized he was staring at me.

"Not on your life," I sneered. "Who's next?"

"We didn't get you anything *tangible*, per se," Goober said from his perch on a kitchen barstool. "But Jorge and I have agreed to hang your Christmas lights this year – *on the house.*"

"And in the bushes, too," Jorge joked from an adjacent stool. His once sallow, alcoholic face now had a healthy glow about it. His brown doe eyes were clear, but still bashful. After locking onto mine for a millisecond, they quickly looked away. "That is, if you want," he added.

"Aww," I cooed. "You two don't have to do that!"

"It was either the lights or a pair of bedroom slippers I found in the dumpster last week," Goober deadpanned. "And I have to say, I've gotten quite attached to the slippers. They're pretty comfy."

I shook my head. "Thanks, guys. I'll take the lights. And Jorge?"

I waited for Jorge to look up at me. "Good luck on your tests on Monday. We're all rooting for you."

"Here here!" Goober and Tom said.

"We know you'll do great," I said. "Good luck to our friend Jorge!"

A round of cheers and cat calls broke out. The warm smile on Jorge's face could have melted a glacier. Then Jorge lowered his eyes again. "Thanks, everybody. I'll do my best."

"That's all anybody can do," Laverne said.

"Absolutely," Cold Cuts agreed, then turned to me. "Well, like the guys, I'm sort of short on cash, too." The cute, bohemian young woman sat cross-legged on the floor beside me, dressed in a pair of leggings and a flowy top that looked as if it had been made from a dozen old scarves. "But I can give you a free makeover for your birthday. How's that?"

"The sooner the better!" Winky cackled.

I shot Winky a sneer, then reached over and hugged the oddball friend I'd made last year while searching for the lost ashes of my biological mom, Glad Goldrich. "Sounds great, Cold Cuts. That would be awesome. Geeze, it seems like ages since I've seen you."

"Been busy with some movie projects," she said, and ran a hand through her carefree, short brown hair. "It's kept me on the road a lot."

"Well, I guess that's good, business wise. So, how's the old RV doing?"

"Actually, she's running like a charm."

"Enough of your gabbing!" Winky hollered from across my small living room. "Open our present next." He leaned over in the lawn chair he'd confiscated from the backyard and smiled at his girlfriend, Winnie. When he squeezed Winnie's hand, her soft, chubby face glowed with a simple contentedness that made me envious.

"Okay, already," I said. "Pass it over."

Tom handed me a package the size of a deck of cards. It was wrapped in Sunday comics and duct tape. The hairs on the back of my neck suddenly pricked up. I shot Winky a wary glare. "What is it?" I asked.

"Well, open the darn thing and find out," Winky said.

I looked over at Winnie. Her expectant face read more like Mother Teresa than the Unabomber, so I tore open the wrapping paper. Inside was a pair of earrings made from fishing tackle. A delighted smile surprised my lips. "Wow!" I held the earrings up for everyone to see. "These are really cool!"

"I thought you might like 'em," Winnie beamed proudly. "We're making them and selling them at flea markets now."

"*And* our fine merchandise can be found in such establishments as Old Joe's Bait and Tackle Shack down by Caddy's," Winky added.

"We call them our 'Playing Hooky' line," Winnie said.

"*Playing Hooky*. Get it?" Winky asked.

"Yes," I said dryly. "I get it. Thanks."

"Let me see them," Cold Cuts said, and took the earrings from my hand. "You're right, Val. These *are* seriously cool. In fact, I might be able to use these in an upcoming photo shoot." She turned to Winky and Winnie. "That could get you guys some exposure."

Winky turned to Winnie. "Do we want to be exposed?"

Winnie smiled and nodded her head. "Yes. That's a good thing."

"Well then," Winky said to Cold Cuts, "we'll take us some of that exposure stuff. I got a tackle box full o' earrings in the van. Wanna see?"

"Sure, I'd –"

"Ahem!" Tom said, clearing his throat. "Before you all run off to rifle through fishing tackle, there's one more present I'd like to give Val." Everybody settled back into place as Tom reached in his jacket pocket and handed me an envelope. I opened it, read the card and nearly fell on the floor.

"What? A week at Sunset Sail-Away Beach Resort?"

"Yep," Tom said proudly. "And it starts tomorrow!"

"Oh my lord!" I leaned over and kissed Tom. "This is awesome! But, Tom...I've got to *work*."

"No you don't," Milly piped up coyly. "The paperwork's already done. You've got the week off."

"All right!" I yelled, a little too enthusiastically for Milly's taste. She eyed me dubiously as I scrambled to my feet and practically jumped in Tom's arms. "I...I don't know what to say! This is gonna be fantastic!"

Tom kissed me and smiled in his charming, boyish way. "Thanks," he said aloud, then leaned in and whispered in my ear, "I was hoping you'd say that."

"LOOKS LIKE THE WHOLE gang made it for your birthday," Tom said as we sorted through the after-party mess in the kitchen.

"Not quite. Mr. Fellows didn't make it."

"You invited your dead parents' attorney?"

I swatted Tom playfully on the butt with a dishtowel. "You know he's more than that. Even though we haven't seen him in a while, he's still my friend. Actually, I'm kind of worried about him. I wonder why he didn't show up."

"Maybe he got a better offer," Tom joked.

I sneered. "Maybe *I'll* get a better offer."

"Not likely," Tom said. He wrapped his strong hands gently around my waist. "At least not in the next thirty minutes."

"I wouldn't be so sure about that," I teased. "So what's your offer?"

Tom brushed his cheek next to mine and whispered words that set my ears and a few other strategic places pulsing with heat. He made good on his offer, too. Let me put it this way; my first unofficial night of being fifty years old was put to good use. In fact, it might have been one for the record books....

I'D SURVIVED TURNING fifty. But not everybody had. When I went out to get the Sunday paper the following morning, there was a dead possum splayed out in the yard like a drunk party guest. Its belly was bloated to the size of a cantaloupe, and its face was smeared with what I hoped was chocolate icing....

Poor old thing, I thought. *Done in by Laverne's cake. Still, better you than me, buddy. Better you than me.*

Chapter Five

A poisoned possum wasn't the only unexpected visitor I discovered in my front yard the morning after my birthday party. Parked at the end of the driveway like a lost wagon from a traveling carny show was a rough-around-the-edges old RV. Cold Cuts had camped out in my driveway overnight.

"Hiya, Val," Cold Cuts called out as I bent over in my nightgown to pick up the Sunday paper. Her unexpected greeting startled me so badly I nearly toppled over head first.

"What are you doing here?" I asked after making a less-than-graceful recovery.

"Sleeping it off," she called back. She stuck her pretty, youthful face out the driver's side window of the old Minnie Winnie. "Had a couple too many beers last night. But I'm good now. Getting ready to take off."

"Oh. Well...wait. Come in and have a coffee."

"What? Are you sure?"

"Yeah. Tom's up. And I want to find out what you've been doing since I last saw you. We didn't get much of a chance to talk last night."

"But you've got your beach resort thing..."

"We're not in any hurry. We can't check in until after 2 p.m., anyway. And the place is just an hour drive from here."

Cold Cuts clicked open the RV door, then hesitated. "Are you sure you're sure?"

"Yes. Why? You don't want to?"

"It's just that...well, in my line of work I'm not used to nude scenes before breakfast." Cold Cuts directed her eyes from my face to my chest, then back.

I looked down. My left boob was hanging out of my nightgown for the whole neighborhood to see. "Arrghh! Why didn't you tell me?" I groaned, and put an end to my public display of indecency.

"I thought you'd figure it out soon enough. But thanks for the morning peep show," Cold Cuts grinned.

I shook my head. "Get inside or get going."

Cold Cuts laughed and climbed out of the RV. "You're in a good mood for turning fifty," she said as she followed me into the house.

She was right. I felt great. Tom and I had a whole week of vacation ahead of us. And we'd started it with two of my favorite things – sleeping in and cappuccinos in bed. "I guess I've got no complaints," I said.

As I led Cold Cuts through the living room to the kitchen, I could see Tom through the sliding glass door. He was in the backyard, shirtless, wiping down the tiki hut bar and talking on his cellphone.

"That's some hot cabana boy you got there," Cold Cuts quipped.

"Yeah. Not bad for an old fart." I pulled a can of coffee from the kitchen cupboard.

"Old fart my boney behind! You two are ageless, I'm telling you."

I shot her an unconvinced sneer. "Uh huh. The coffee's free. You don't need to butter me up."

Cold Cuts smirked. "Well, since you're on to my game, I was aiming for a Pop-Tart."

I laughed and clicked the coffee on to perk. I grabbed two cartons of Pop-Tarts out of the cabinet. "Pick your poison. Strawberry or blueberry?"

"Ooooh. Blueberry, please!"

Cold Cuts' open enthusiasm was so childlike, I almost felt like her mother. "Coming right up, then." I reached to plug the toaster into its usual socket, but my efforts were thwarted by a strip of duct tape. "Oh yeah," I muttered.

"Too bad about your ring," Cold Cuts said. "I wanted to see it."

I shrugged. "You will, soon enough." I found another outlet and plugged the toaster in. "Have a seat."

Cold Cuts climbed onto a barstool at the kitchen counter.

"So, how's the disguise biz going?" I asked as I popped two tarts into the toaster.

"Slow, but steady. Not complaining. You know, I still think about our Date Busters days."

"Oh geeze. Don't remind me. You in that dumb clown getup...and the rainbow Mohawk chick. Who could forget that?" I pushed down the toaster lever.

"And Milly, the trailer-trash prom queen – complete with tiara," Cold Cuts snickered.

"Tsk...amateur," I sneered and shook my head playfully, then grabbed a mug from the cupboard and picked up the coffee carafe.

"Oh! Oh!" Cold Cuts cried, wiggling on her stool like the class know-it-all. "I have to tell you this, Val!"

"What?"

"I was working on the set of a nude scene last week, and all I could think about was that time Milly was in the RV. You know, the time when she put that pubic wig on her face and wore it like a beard!"

"Oh my word!" I said, my hand poised to pour the coffee. "Poor Milly. I thought she was going to lose it."

Cold Cuts jumped off the stool and ran around, flailing her arms wildly. "Help! Get it off me, get it off me!"

"Ha ha! The merkin jerk!" I laughed so hard I splashed more coffee onto the counter than into the mug. "Poor Milly....she's sworn me to secrecy on that one, you know."

"Who could blame her?" Cold Cuts snickered and sat back on her stool. She glanced at the mess I'd made. "You'd never make it as a waitress," she said as I wiped up the spilled coffee.

"Believe it or not, I've been told that before."

I handed her the mug of coffee and the toaster popped up.

"Right on cue," Cold Cuts said.

I put the pastries on a plate and was in the middle of handing them to Cold Cuts when Tom shrieked out my name. Startled, I dropped the plate. Cold Cuts made a quick save.

"What's going on?" she asked.

"I dunno!"

"Val!" Tom called again from the back door. He stumbled into the kitchen, his face marred with concern.

"What's wrong?" I asked.

"Goober just called. Jorge's having a meltdown."

"What do you mean, Tom? What happened?"

"*Winky* happened, that's what," Tom snapped. "Goober told me Winky found Jorge at the dining room table, asleep over his study papers."

"So?"

"Well, Winky thought he'd have a little fun waking him up."

My face filled with dread. "Uh oh."

"Exactly," Tom said. "According to Goober, Winky sneaked up behind Jorge and tapped him on the shoulder. When he woke up and turned around, Winky was standing there in a ski mask. He shot Jorge in the face with a water pistol."

"Oh no!" I cried. "What happened?"

Tom shook his head. "Jorge punched Winky in the face, then locked himself in the bathroom. Goober said it's like 'babysitting a barroom brawl' over there right now."

"When are those guys ever gonna grow up?"

"Probably never," Tom said. "Geeze. I really want Jorge to get back on his feet."

"We all do."

Tom looked me in the eye and his face softened. "Yeah, I know. But Val, all that pressure of the exams tomorrow. It's bad enough for a *normal*...." Tom stopped himself. "You know what I mean. I'm not sure Jorge can take it. Not with those bozos over there making things even harder for him."

"What can I do?" I asked.

Tom looked me in the eye. "I hate to say it, Val, but...I think I should stay with him. Just through the exams. Would you be upset if I didn't –"

"Oh, crap, Tom! I don't want to go to the beach *without* you."

"It's too late to cancel the reservations, Val. It would be a waste for someone not to go."

"That really sucks," Cold Cuts said.

I'd forgotten she was there. I looked over just in time to see her take a big bite of Pop-tart.

"*I* know," Tom said to Cold Cuts. "Why don't *you* go in my place?"

"What?" Cold Cuts mumbled through a mouthful of Pop-tart.

"Just for a day or two," Tom explained. He turned back to face me. "Jorge's exams are tomorrow, Val. I could try to come after that, or first thing the next morning."

"Tom...," I started.

"This is important, Val. You know as well as I do I can't leave Jorge to fend for himself over there."

My gut slumped. "I know. You're right." I turned to Cold Cuts. "Are you free? Can you come?"

Cold Cuts showed us her blueberry-stained teeth. "Sure. I can do it."

"Okay, then," I said. A thought hit me. "But crap! How would we get there? I'm afraid to drive Shabby Maggie. She's been acting up lately."

"No problem," Cold Cuts said between slurps of coffee. "We can take Glad's trusty old RV."

"ROAD TRIP!" COLD CUTS cheered as the vintage RV coughed and sputtered its way out of my driveway.

"Are you sure the old girl can make it?" I asked as I looked in the vanity mirror. The earrings from Winnie and Winky dangled from my lobes.

"Sure. She's just a little cranky in the morning."

"I can understand that. I hope she can make it over the Sunshine Skyway Bridge."

"She's done it before," Cold Cuts said, and patted the dashboard. "Just need to make sure she's only half full of gas."

Great. "Once you get to the next stop sign, turn left."

"I've got this, Val. Relax. I've been down to Sarasota a time or two."

"Oh. Okay, then. I'll leave you to it." I looked out the window and watched Laverne's house slowly disappear. "Hey. Since you've got it all under control, do you mind if I just take a look around in the back? For old time's sake?"

Cold Cuts smiled. "Knock yourself out."

I squeezed Cold Cuts shoulder as I climbed out of my seat, then fumbled through the short hallway into the main cabin of the RV. It was almost unrecognizable from when I'd last seen it. Cold Cuts had painted the old brown paneling a cool, apple green. Bags full of costumes and wigs and shoes hung from hooks along the walls, crowding the already tiny space as they swayed gently in tune with the motion of Cold Cuts' hand on the steering wheel.

Curious, I opened a small cabinet above the tiny, two-burner stove. A glittery dragonfly sticker stared back at me from the inside corner of the cupboard door. Like a magical time portal, the dragonfly triggered a flashback to the first time I'd stepped foot inside the RV. At the time, the old Minnie Winnie had been wedged in amongst a mountain of trashed appliances and household rubbish in the backyard of a house owned by a dead hoarder named Tony Goldrich. It was part of the lifetime of accumulated detritus left behind by him and his wife, Gladys.

Back then, nearly every surface of the old RV's interior had been plastered with stickers and magazine cutouts of dragonflies. Gladys had gone a little nuts over losing their only child. But, thinking back on it now, I don't think she ever gave up hope of finding her one day. Why else would she have left a thousand crazy clues all over the place? The dragonflies were little beacons, staring anyone in the face who was determined enough to put two-and-two together.

As fate would have it, that person had been me.

Against all odds, I'd been given a chance to get to know Gladys (Glad) Goldrich before she'd died. I'd literally stumbled upon her at Sunset Beach, just when I'd desperately needed a friend. She been that for me with no reservations – despite the fact that I, at first, avoided her like the plague. She'd worn down my resistance with her unshakeable good humor and total acceptance of me, warts and all.

A sudden realization sent a chill down my spine. *If she hadn't reached out, I wouldn't have. And I wouldn't be standing here now.*

If Glad hadn't spoken to me that fateful Mother's Day, I'd have never gotten to know her. And I'd have never cared enough about her to go rifling through her things after she and her husband died. I'd have never found that broken piece of a dragonfly pendant. I'd have never discovered that their long-lost daughter was actually *me*....

My fingers found the dragonfly pendant on the chain around my neck and thought of Glad. My skin prickled to gooseflesh, and an image of Glad at the beach overwhelmed my mind. There she was, a skinny old lady with arms and legs as dark and leathery as Slim Jims, sprawled out in that cheap pink beach lounger of hers. Those red, lipstick-smeared lips smiling at me. The reflection of the sun and sand shining from her black, bug-eyed sunglasses.

In my mind, she hoisted a quart-sized can of Fosters in the air and said, "Screw you, kiddo!"

I twirled the dragonfly pendant between my fingers, then let it go. "I miss you, Glad," I whispered.

"Hey, what's going on back there?" Cold Cuts called out from the driver's cabin. "Mitts off the merkins!"

I smiled, kissed my fingertip and touched it to the glittery dragonfly sticker. As I closed the cabinet door I whispered, "Thanks for leading me to a new friend, mom."

Chapter Six

"Whoa, man, this place is *swanky!*" Cold Cuts said as we pulled up to the 'Guest Arrival Center' at the Sunset Sail-Away Beach Resort. She cut the ignition. The old RV shuddered, belched black smoke and coughed itself out.

"I know," I said. "It actually *looks* like the webpage. That's a first."

Cold Cuts twisted her upper lip. "Geeze. If I'd known how *nice* this place was, I'd have taken the old gal through a car wash first."

"Oh my!" I said, looking past Cold Cuts through the driver's side window pane.

A young, tan, Brad Pitt lookalike in a Hawaiian shirt and khaki shorts walked up and tapped on Cold Cut's window.

"Hello, ladies! May I help you with your luggage?"

Cold Cuts gave him a quick once-over and turned to me and said, "I like this place already. Look, Val, all my stuff's in the back. Stall this guy, would you, while I throw a bag together?"

"No problem." I motioned to the young Adonis. "Meet me at the side door." He nodded and I ambled over to the place I'd stowed my old blue suitcase. Meanwhile, Cold Cuts scurried around in the cabin, picking through bags and digging through drawers like a robber high on Red Bull and crack.

My old suitcase looked dirty and scuffed and not up to snuff as I handed it to the shiny, ridiculously handsome young porter. If he thought so, too, he didn't let on one iota.

"And the other young lady?" he asked as he set the suitcase down on the ground beside him. He tried to peek inside the RV, but I stepped out and closed the side door behind me.

"She'll be coming in a minute," I said to him cheerfully. "So, where do we check in?"

"Follow me, beautiful," the suave Chippendales shoo-in said, and flashed me another of his devastating smiles. If I'd had a nickel between my teeth, I'd have bitten right through it.

He led me through a pair of carved mahogany doors that soared ten feet high. Inside, the lobby looked like something out of a 1950's film involving Elvis and Hawaii. Comfy-looking rattan chairs and sofas upholstered in tropical fabrics were nestled in groups around potted palms and bamboo cocktail tables. The walls were covered in vintage Hawaiian memorabilia and retro paintings of surfers hanging ten off crystal blue, churning waves as high as mountains. Nothing about the place said "Florida." But what the heck. I saw Florida every day.

"Here we are," the porter said. "The reception desk. Monty will take good care of you, now." He flashed his diamond smile at me patiently and steadily, until I got the hint and pressed a five-dollar bill into his palm. "Thank you, miss," the porter said, and winked. Being called 'miss' instead of 'ma'am' had been worth the entire fiver.

"Good afternoon! Don't you look lovely," Monty the desk clerk said in the posh, English accent of a snooty butler on PBS. Probably in his early forties, the thin, balding man's voice denoted a cheerfulness so practiced and smooth I almost fell for it. "You must be Ms. Foreman?"

"Fremden," I corrected with a weak smile.

"Oh. Pardon me," Monty said. He flashed a pained, uneven-toothed smile that added credibility to the case for him being authentically British. Unlike the porter, Monty was dressed primly in a dark blue business suit. "I hope you found young Brad's services up to your standards."

"His name is *Brad?*"

"Yes, miss. Is that a problem? We can change it."

"No. Not at all."

"Good. We have you and your partner in cottage number 22, the honeymoon cabana. Congratulations on your impending nuptials."

"What?" I said, my gut suddenly tightening. "Wait a minute. We're not getting –"

"Oh, come on, sugar!" Cold Cuts' voice rang out behind me. Her slender hand inched around my waist. "We don't have to pretend *here*."

Dumbfounded, my lips scrunched together and nearly met my nose. But I kept my mouth shut. Monty smiled at us as if we were the cutest pair of puppies he'd ever seen. Then he looked down at his computer and said, "Hmmm."

My mind played a sound like a needle scratching across spinning vinyl.

"My apologies, ladies. There seems to be a problem with your room. It's not quite...ready."

I let out a sigh big enough to blow up a balloon.

Cold Cuts kissed me on the cheek. "Aww, honey, it'll be all right."

Monty shot me a quick glance and looked back down at his computer. He punched a few buttons. "Did I say problem? My mistake, ladies! There are no 'problems' at the Sunset Sail-Away Beach Resort. Only happy-day solutions."

I threw up a little in my mouth. Eagle-eyed Monty noticed. He switched the focus of his sugary placations to the customer in front of him who appeared more receptive. "Miss Foreman?" he asked Cold Cuts.

"Sure," Cold Cuts said with a smirk.

"On behalf of Sunset Sail-Away Beach Resort, I'd like to offer you and your...uh, *partner*...complimentary cocktails at the beachside cabana bar," Monty said. "Please, allow us the honor of preparing your room as you while away an hour strolling the white-sand beach with your favorite libation. Sound good?"

Cold Cuts elbowed me and whispered, "Libation, huh? That's a funny name for a porter."

"What was that, miss?" Monty asked.

"Sounds fantastic," Cold Cuts said. Monty smiled that painful smile again and went back to fiddling with the computer.

"Behave!" I whispered to Cold Cuts. "The porter's name is Brad."

"You're kidding."

"Nope."

"Very good, then," Monty said. "It's all arranged. Here are your free cocktail passes." He slid two tokens across the reception desk toward us.

Cold Cuts grabbed the tokens. "So, Monty, can we stow our luggage with you?"

"Certainly, miss."

"Thanks. Here you go." Cold Cuts reached over the reception desk and handed Monty two plastic grocery bags stuffed with who knows what. From one bag, a pair of pink panties clung precariously to a squashed tube of toothpaste.

Monty smiled weakly. "Very good, miss." He reached out and took each bag between a pinched thumb and index finger like a well-dressed, fastidious crab.

I stifled a smirk and bobbed my head to the left. "My suitcase is over there. The blue one."

Monty gamboled a quick glance at my beat-up case. With Herculean effort, he managed an ingratiating fake smile. "Perfect. I'll shall see to your luggage, ladies. Please enjoy your time at the cabana bar. You'll find it out those doors." Monty motioned with his head, since his hands were fully occupied holding sacks of Cold Cuts' unmentionables. "Simply follow the path toward the beach. You can't miss it."

"Thank you, Monty," Cold Cuts said sweetly. "And please, be careful with my luggage. It's a matched set, you know."

"YOU ARE ROTTEN TO THE core, Cold Cuts!" I laughed as the lobby door closed behind us.

"You love it, Admit it!" she giggled. She stuck her nose in the air in an imitation of Monty. "Very good, miss!"

"Okay. I admit it." I snickered. I took a deep breath and let the sweet, salty smell of the Gulf of Mexico fill my lungs. "Ahhh! We're here!"

"We sure are," Cold Cuts agreed.

I studied her for a moment, and a sudden wave envious nostalgia washed over me. Cold Cuts reminded me of myself – albeit, a thinner, twenty-year younger version. "I'm looking forward to getting to know you better," I said.

"I should hope so," she winked. "After all, we're on our honeymoon."

"Pardon me, ladies," Brad the porter said as he rushed by, heading for the cabana bar.

I rolled my eyes. "Great. So, what do you want to do now?"

"I don't know about you," Cold Cuts said, "but I envision a margarita in my near future."

I grinned. "Funny you should say that. I had the same premonition."

I followed Cold Cuts along a winding, sandy path that cut through a veritable forest of tropical foliage. On either side of the main path, every thirty feet or so, we saw side trails numbered with little wooden signs. Some offered scattered glimpses of thatched roof cottages tucked away in their own lush, private settings. Soon, we were so close to the Gulf I could hear the gentle surf and the sharp cries of seagulls.

"How romantic!" Cold Cuts said, trying to peek over a hibiscus hedge. "This really *is* the perfect place for a honeymoon."

"Honeymoon," said a man's gravelly voice behind us.

Startled, I twirled around. Standing less than two feet away was a man dressed from head to toe in what appeared to be some pretty serious fishing attire. Atop his head was a floppy hat with a shroud of netting obscuring his face like a beekeeper's getup. Khaki-colored pants and a long-sleeved shirt covered everything else but his bare hands and feet. The pockets of his camouflage vest poked out as if stuffed to the gills with cotton. A red tackle box hung from one hand, a fishing rod from the other. He could have been mistaken for an ichthyologist from planet Redneckopia.

"Hello," I offered. "Are you staying here?"

"Hard-bodied grubs," the man muttered, then pushed past us and disappeared into the dense foliage.

"Weird," I said.

"*Really* weird," Cold Cuts concurred. "And rude, *I think*.... I mean, did he just insult us?"

"Well, he did say *hard-bodied*. I'll take that as a compliment."

Cold Cuts smirked. "Fair enough. And the grubs?"

I thought about Brad and Monty. "Well, compared to the other folks around here, that isn't too off the mark."

Cold Cuts laughed. "Maybe you're right. But it's still weird as crap."

I shrugged in agreement. "Why does everything weird always happen to *me?*"

"Just lucky, I guess," Cold Cuts said.

"Yeah. Lucky me." I took a step toward the cabana bar. "I am *sooo* ready for that drink."

Chapter Seven

E ven paradise had fleas.

I was at an awesomely cool cabana bar on the beach with a friend. The day was gorgeous, the drinks were free, and all I could think about was something that had been bugging me since Cold Cuts and I had first arrived at the resort. I'd vowed not to let it bother me, but like that lone mosquito buzzing around your face in the dark, it's always the little things that get to you in the end. A couple of shots of tequila erased what was left of my resolve to keep my trap shut. That darn Jose Cuervo always had a way of loosening my lips.

"That guy thought we were married...er...I mean, that we were *getting* married," I said to Cold Cuts from my barstool. I caught the bartender's eye. "Another round, please."

"What are you talking about?" Cold Cuts asked, and twirled on her barstool to face me. Clothed in a sort-of ratty t-shirt and stretchy workout pants, my young friend looked sexier than I felt in my nice jeans and turquois, button-down blouse.

"At the reception desk. Monty. He congratulated me on our impending nuptials."

"Yeah. I heard. So what?"

"What do you think he meant? You don't think Tom was planning on springing a *wedding* on me while we're here, do you?"

Cold Cuts choked on her margarita. "You make it sound like a *bad* thing. I mean, aren't you already engaged?"

I frowned. "Yeah. It's just that –"

"Relax, Val. I think you're reading way too much into it. That guy Monty's a screw-up. He can't even get our room right. He probably got you mixed up with someone else."

"You think?"

"Yeah. Probably. But the real question is, why are you so scared of getting married?"

I took a long draw on my second margarita. "No. The *real* question is, why *aren't* you?"

Cold Cuts laughed. "You know how I feel about this already, Val. I don't see marriage as the 'til death-sentence do we part' kind a deal like you do. It's more like, I dunno, a *consensual merging of two lives*. I mean, people come into your life for a *reason*, you know. When that reason is over, it's time for them to go."

"Yeah, that sounds good and all. But what if *you're* ready for them to go, but *they* don't want to?"

Cold Cuts grinned like a cute little Yoda. "Well, that's kind of the best part. The way I see it, *that* can't happen. Our thoughts and feelings – they're like magnets, Val. They attract people and experiences to us, or repel them away. When it comes down to it, *we're* the ones who decide what's gonna happen in our lives."

"Yeah, you've told me that before," I said, suddenly feeling a lot more sober than I wanted to. "But it's hard to believe. I mean, I don't *want* to be responsible for attracting all the crap that's happened in my life."

Cold Cuts laughed. "What crap? There *is no crap*, Val. *Every* experience has value. If we're smart, we use the painful stuff to point us in a new direction. You know, toward something better – something we want more."

"This is all too much after two margaritas." I sucked my margarita glass dry with a loud slurp.

"Well, how about looking at it this way," Cold Cuts said. "If you could live your life over again, what would you change? Just keep in mind, every alteration would also change who you are right now."

My thoughts swam around the idea like a fly in a martini.

"So?" Cold Cuts repeated. "What would you change?"

I hiccoughed. "Can I ask for no cellulite?"

Cold Cuts laughed and made a buzzer sound. "Eeennnkk. Irrelevant, Val. You are *not* defined by your cellulite."

"Tell that to *Vogue*."

"I'm not talking about your *body*. I'm talking about your *essence*, Val. Your *soul*. Whatever you want to call it. If you could, would you want to be someone different than who you are now?"

The waiter set a fresh margarita in front of me. I eyed it, then turned to Cold Cuts.

"It might be the margaritas talking, but I guess I'd say 'no.' The crap I've been through...well, it's made me realize I'm one tough old gal."

"How so?" Cold Cuts asked, and licked a bit of salt from the rim of her glass.

"I dunno. Even if I can't count on other people, I know I can count on *me*, no matter what. I've pulled myself up by my bootstraps enough times to know *that*, if nothing else. So, if it's like you say, that my experiences made me who I am...I guess I'd have to say 'no,' I wouldn't change a thing. Not a darn thing."

Cold Cuts stopped sipping her margarita and shot me a huge grin. "Good. Because I wouldn't either. I think you're perfect just the way you are."

"Who are you? Mr. Darcy reincarnated?"

Cold Cuts crinkled her nose? "Who's Mr. Darcy?"

I sighed. "Never mind."

"All I'm saying, Val, is *believe* what you just told me. Believe that you are who you are right now because that's who you *choose* to be. Relax. Trust yourself. Whatever you decide – about Tom or even what to eat for dinner tonight – *it's all good*. It's all part of the plan. So lighten up. Enjoy yourself!"

I stared in amazement at the cute, brunette Buddha on a barstool. "Geeze. I wish I had your confidence when I was your age."

Cold Cuts tipped her head. "Thanks."

"I wish I had your *thighs* right now."

Cold Cuts laughed. "I'm happy with who I am, Val. But if I was you, I'd be just as happy."

I shook my head. "How is that *possible?*"

"Because it isn't the shape of your thighs or the thickness of your wallet that determines your happiness," Cold Cuts said. "No matter where you are or who you're with, happiness is *a choice*. I choose to be happy. And I think you do too, in your own weirdly wonderful way."

"All right already." I climbed off my barstool and wobbled to standing. "Before you make me cry or bust a blood vessel in my brain, I'm gonna go check to see if the room is ready."

"Okay," Cold Cuts said. "Hug first." She hopped off her barstool and hugged me tight.

"You'll be okay on your own?" I asked.

"Sure. Don't you worry about me." Cold Cuts glanced across the bar at a cute guy. "I'll figure out something to do until you get back."

MONTY DIDN'T LOOK TOO thrilled to see me.

"I'm sorry ma...uh...*miss*," he said, his British accent seeming to fail him for a moment. He quickly plastered over the crack in his thin veneer of hospitality. "There's been a slight...um...*delay*."

"You're kidding." Two and a half margaritas in my bloodstream – and the news of no bed to lie down on – suddenly made me desperate for a nap.

Monty looked down at his computer and punched some buttons. "I assure you, Ms. Fremden, your room will be ready soon." He reached over the registration desk and slid a couple of plastic, credit-card-looking things toward me. "Please, enjoy these free passes to the fitness and spa facilities. A relaxation yoga class is beginning in the Pagoda Room in fifteen minutes. I *highly* recommend it."

"Excuse me, Monty," I crabbed. "Do I *look* like I need relaxation yoga?"

"Why of course not, miss!"

Uh huh. It's official. Monty is a big, fat liar.

I FOUND COLD CUTS SITTING alone on her stool, her back to the otherwise empty cabana bar. She was facing the beach, but her eyes were closed. The late afternoon sun illuminated her serene, young face with touches of warm pink. The salty breeze tousled her short, brown hair. The only sounds were the surf and a distant seagull cry. The scene was so perfect, it stopped me in my tracks. Loathe to disturb it, I took a faltering step back and stubbed my heel on a coconut.

"Ouch!"

Cold Cuts stirred from her picture-postcard vignette. "Hey."

"What happened to the hot guy?" I said sheepishly. "I figured you'd be under a beach umbrella making out by now."

Cold Cuts shrugged. "Married."

"Oh. Well, that's strike two, I'm afraid. Our room's still not ready. But I got these as a consolation prize." I dumped the two cards on the bar. "Spa passes. There's a yoga class starting in like...ten minutes."

Cold Cuts smiled good-naturedly. "Oh. That's okay. Hey, it's not like we're in a big hurry. Let's try the yoga class. What the heck."

"Sure," I groused. "Nothing like doing yoga half lit. In jeans."

"Those look like stretch jeans. Am I right?"

I raised a disgruntled eyebrow. "And your point is?"

"Uh...they stretch?"

I scowled. "They're not *that* stretchy."

"Oh come on." Cold Cuts hopped off her bar stool and tugged on my arm. Begrudgingly, I followed her away from free drinks at the tiki bar toward a place I'd pay good money *not* to visit.

"This is supposed to be a *vacation*," I groused.

"A little yoga never hurt anybody."

"Well, there's always a *first time*."

I was tipsy and sleepy and pouting like a spoiled brat when Cold Cuts finally figured out where the Pagoda Room was. When we went inside, the room was empty.

I smiled. "Oh, too bad. Let's go."

Cold Cuts laughed. "Don't be so grouchy. If nobody shows by 4 p.m. on the dot, I promise we'll go. Deal?"

I sighed in lieu of an answer. Cold Cuts leaned against a wall and began stretching her legs. I flopped into a folding chair by the door and watched the second hand sweep around the clock four times with the anticipation of a death-row inmate on execution day. At three seconds to 4 p.m., I shot Cold Cuts a snotty victory grin, stood up and reached for the doorknob. As if by some demonic force, it turned on its own.

The door flew open. The man standing there looked almost as startled as I did. "Ladies," he said, "Welcome to Relaxation Yoga with Guru Bill."

Dressed in off-white, loose-fitting linen pants and a matching, sack-like, long-sleeved shirt, the slender man appeared to be in his mid-thirties. But it was hard to tell. His entire face, with the exception of his nose, eyes and forehead, were covered in thick, dark-brown hair. Even the toes of his bare feet sprouted an impressive patch of hair. Given his long beard and the thick mane of hair that flowed past his shoulders, I might have mistaken him for Jesus – if I'd been hopped up on Nyquil.

"Are you fit enough for this?" our savior of the yoga mat asked me. "Your face is flushed."

"She's fit enough," Cold Cuts vouched. "It's not high blood pressure. It's tequila."

"Oh. In that case, let's get started," Bill said without so much as a wayward blink. "Everyone grab a yoga mat."

I walked over and tugged a thin, rubbery mat from a pile in the corner. It was curled up like a purple cinnamon roll and smelled like old gym socks. The tacky way it stuck to itself as I unrolled it made my skin crawl.

Guru Bill smiled serenely. "Now, lay down on your mats."

Ugh. Thankfully, the tequila had loosened me up. I lay down, feeling like a kindergartener at nap time. Bill sat cross-legged on the floor and began to chant. I started to doze off. *Hey, this isn't so bad....*

"The first posture is called downward dog," Bill said, startling me out of my semi-conscious daze. "Roll over on your stomachs."

I opened my eyes. Guru Bill had fashioned his thick head of hair into a man-bun the size of a small planet. He'd also taken off his shirt, revealing a thin, surprisingly hairless torso. A pair of gold rings hung from his small, brown nipples, making me wonder if he might have a side job as a human curtain-rod holder.

"Oh. I forgot the music," he said.

To my amazement, he rose to his feet, straight up from his cross-legged position, like some ethereal entity. As he walked over to a boom box, I turned my head and whispered to Cold Cuts.

"Look at that. Nipple piercings!"

She grinned back at me coyly. "I kinda like 'em."

"Are you nuts? What's up with your generation?"

"What's up with yours?" Cold Cuts' eyebrows knitted together, her face more curious than judgmental. "What's so wrong with tattoos and piercings? It's not like you take your body with you when you go."

"Well, thank goodness for that."

"Ahem," Guru Bill said.

We looked up to find Bill staring at us blankly. "Ladies, yoga is all about mind-body connection and flow," he said. "Talking anchors you within your head and keeps you out of the flow. Silence, please. Let me return us to flow."

Bill sat down on the mat and folded his legs again like a Buddha statue. He closed his eyes, took a deep breath and belted out a reverberating, "Oooohhhmmmm" sound that he kept up for what seemed like five minutes.

I whispered to Cold Cuts during his one-note opera, "*That* doesn't count as talking?" I glanced at Bill. He was shutting one slightly peeved eye.

That concluded the relaxation part of the class. For the next thirty minutes, Bill the masochist guru had us contorting our bodies into triangles, pretzels and crescent shapes. Shockingly, I'd survived everything he'd thrown at us until he instructed us stand against the wall, bend at the waist and hang our heads. When I did, a strange sensation crawled along my crotch and up my backside.

Oh crap! My jeans had run out of stretch and ripped halfway up my butt. Thankfully, from my position against a wall, this could remain, for the moment, my little secret.

"Now we will conclude with shavasina," Guru Bill said. "Lay on your backs on your mats."

The last thing I remembered was Bill rubbing a stick around the rim of a metal bowl. Then Cold Cuts shook my shoulder.

"Class is over, Val. Wake up."

"Huh?" I lifted myself onto an elbow and wiped drool from the corner of my mouth. "Must have been the margaritas." A cool breeze behind me reminded me I'd split my jeans. "I think I'll just lay here a minute."

"You okay?" Cold Cuts asked.

"Yeah, fine."

"Many people find deep release with yoga," Bill said, his linen-covered form suddenly appearing over me like a hairy-faced ghost. "You're one of the lucky ones."

"Uh...thanks," I replied.

He knelt beside me and handed me a business card. "If you're interested in a personal consultation while you're here, I'm available on an appointment basis."

I held the card up to my bleary eyes. "Bill Robo. Ka' Manawa Nalaya Personal Yoga Instruction and Massage. What does Ka' Manawa Nalaya mean?" I asked.

"I completed my yoga training in Hawaii."

"Which island?" Cold Cuts asked.

"Uh...the big one," he said, and stood up.

"Uh huh," I said. "Mind if I just lay here another minute?"

"Not at all," Bill said, and turned his attention to Cold Cuts. "Here. A card for you as well, Darling Faun. Just so you know, I make cottage calls."

Cold Cuts took the card. I noticed his hand linger on hers and their eyes lock. "Call me," I heard him whisper. Then he folded his hands as if in prayer, bowed at me and padded barefoot out of the room.

"Come on, *Darling Faun*," I sneered. "Let's go see if our room is ready." I hauled myself to standing.

"You don't think he's kinda cute?" Cold Cuts asked as she rolled up her mat.

"Didn't you see his card? Ka' Manawa Nalaya? Give me a break!"

"What?"

"Come on, I wanna lay ya?"

"Oh." Cold Cuts burst out laughing. "Well, you gotta give him points for originality."

"How can you say that? The guy's a fraud!"

"You don't know that."

"No offense, but I'm pretty sure I saw him on the side of the road last week holding a sign that read, 'Will work for mushrooms.'"

Cold Cuts laughed. "You did not!"

"Pretty sure," I said, and bent over to roll up my yoga mat.

"Uh, Val, your pants are split."

"Yes, I'm aware of that fact. And I need you to cover for me."

"What do you mean?"

"When we leave, stay close behind me. So nobody can see. Okay?"

Cold Cuts grinned. "Got it."

Chapter Eight

C old Cuts shadowed behind me and my ripped jeans like a too-friendly dancer in a conga line. She was doing her best to cover my embarrassing southern exposure, but her enthusiastic silliness was making me feel even more embarrassed. When we stopped at the reception desk, she snuggled up against my back, propped her head on my shoulder and wrapped her arms around my waist.

"My apologies again," Monty said, looking up slowly. I noticed his haughty face appeared strained. He shot me a brief, tight smile and said, "This is highly unusual, Ms. Fremden, let me assure you."

I wondered if he was talking about us or the room. I glanced at the clock on the wall above Monty's sweating bald head. It was 5:23 p.m.

"Your room should be ready shortly," he said in a voice that belied even *he* had his doubts.

"Look, Monty," I said, then glanced around the room to make sure no one else was watching. "I really need to...uh...change my clothes."

"Yes," Monty said without batting an eyelash. "I understand."

I jerked and squirmed as Cold Cuts tickled my ribcage. "Stop it," I whispered over my shoulder. She kissed me playfully on the cheek.

"We have a *changing room* you could use," Monty offered, averting his eyes. "But it's quite small."

"We'll make it work," Cold Cuts chirped. "Where is it?"

The longsuffering desk clerk pursed his lips and sighed almost imperceptibly. "Down the hall, first door on the left. Here's the key."

I snatched it from his hand. "Thanks. I'll need my suitcase."

"Oh. Yes. Of course. The *blue* one, as I recall." He pushed my mangy case with his foot until it rounded the corner to our side of the reception desk. "When you're through um...*changing your clothes*...we would like to offer you complimentary cocktails and hors d'oeuvres at the cabana bar. And, if you care to, please enjoy a sunset sail with our resident captain. With our compliments, of course."

Cold Cuts giggled like a tipsy schoolgirl as Monty handed me a brochure. On the front was a picture of a gorgeous, twenty-foot sailboat manned by an even more gorgeous, twenty-something man. "This looks really nice," I said.

"Did I mention free cocktails?" Monty asked.

"Yes you did," Cold Cuts said, then pinched me on the bottom. I winced and felt my face heat up like a volcanic eruption.

"I'll be needing my bag, as well," Cold Cuts giggled like a dime-store floozy. "The one with the toothpaste."

"Very good, miss." Monty's head disappeared behind the desk as he bent over. He popped back up holding the grocery bag as if it were the putrid tail of a dead rodent.

Cold Cuts grabbed the bag over my shoulder. "Thank you, Monty dear!"

"I'll bring back the key," I told Monty, then backed slowly away from the reception desk, Cold Cuts hanging on me like a drunken sailor.

"I'll be here," Monty said flatly, and produced a hard, tight smile I'm sure he saved just for such lovely occasions as this.

"WHAT AM I GONNA DO with you?" I asked Cold Cuts as I rifled through my suitcase in a changing room not much bigger than a broom closet.

"Aww, come on. I'm just trying to get you to have some fun. Why are you so cranky?"

I thought about her question for a moment, but no good answer came to mind. "I don't know," I said finally.

"Do you want to do the sunset sail?" Cold Cuts asked and made a face so goofy I forgot to sneer and laughed out loud instead.

"You know what, why not?" I grinned and decided to follow her lead and make the most of the situation. "What should we wear?"

"I'm gonna wear a sundress with my bathing suit on under it." Cold Cuts raised her grubby t-shirt over her head. "I think I'll go for a swim in the moonlight!"

The idea kind of scared me, but I didn't let on. "Good idea," I lied, and picked through my suitcase for my old reliable, one-piece bathing suit. It wasn't in there. All I found instead was that blasted gold thong bikini Laverne had given me for my birthday. I held it up for Cold Cuts to see. "Someone's sabotaged my suitcase."

Cold Cuts laughed. "Well, look on the bright side."

"There's a bright side to this?" I held up the tangle of gold strings and tiny triangles.

"Sure. If you get wet, it'll dry faster."

"Hmmm."

Cold Cuts fastened the hook on a pink bikini top. "And it'll be sunset. Everybody looks better in the twilight."

"You have a point, there," I said, and stripped off my jeans featuring their new, air-conditioned crotch. "Bikinis and sundresses it is."

"And cocktails," Cold Cuts said as she tugged a cute, sky-blue sundress over her head. She smoothed it into place on her torso and cocked an eyebrow at me. "Don't forget the cocktails."

"Believe me, there's no chance of that." I wriggled from the odd sensation of gold string rubbing between my butt cheeks. "Ugh!" I groaned, then pulled a sundress from my suitcase and closed the luggage fasteners. "Could you take the key and my case back to Monty while I finish dressing? I want to take a minute to check in with Tom."

Cold Cuts shrugged. "No problem. As long as you don't need me to dance the Macarena with you anymore."

"Nope. I'm good."

"Meet you at the cabana bar?"

"Yeah," I said, fishing through my purse. "Sounds like a plan."

Cold Cuts picked up her grocery bag and my suitcase, then elbowed the door open. On the way out, she tripped on my shoes and tumbled right into the arms of yoga guru and nipple-ring model, Bill Robo. He raised a bushy eyebrow at us and smiled.

"Having a good time, ladies?" he asked.

"The best," Cold Cuts said, then turned back toward me and blew me a kiss.

It didn't get more humiliating in my book than being suspected of canoodling in a broom closet wearing nothing but a gold thong bikini. "Perfect," I sighed, and gave in to the madness. "Darling, would you please let Monty know we're taking him up on the offer of a sunset sail?"

"Why of course," Cold Cuts and Bill said in unison, then turned and giggled at each other.

I flashed the pair a simpering smile and kicked the closet door closed with my bare foot. As the trail of laughter faded down the hallway, I sat down on a bench and punched #7, speed dial for Tom. It rang three times, then went to his answering machine.

"Hi, Tom. It's me," I said into the phone. "Just wondering how things were going with Jorge and the guys. This place is really nice. We're having fun." The hollowness of my voice caught me off guard, and I found myself adding, "I miss you."

Chapter Nine

As I strolled up to the cabana bar, Cold Cuts was sitting on a barstool again, but this time she wasn't alone. She'd been cornered by a blobby, sweaty-looking man old enough to be her father. His orange sport shirt was blinding. But it still didn't deflect my eyes from the main attraction. Perched atop the ruddy-faced slob's head was either the world's most tragic toupee, or some poor squirrel hadn't saved enough nuts to make it through winter.

Cold Cuts turned toward me as I walked up. Her eyebrows knitted together and she mouthed the words, "Help me!"

"Hi. I'm Jim," the greasy man said. He held out a meaty handful of fat fingers that sent my mind racing back to the time my mother had tried to pass off cigar-shaped globs of Spam as hotdogs. I shook his gross, pink fingers and tried to make a grimace into a smile.

"Hi. I'm Val." I said, then glanced around the bar for a Wet-Wipe.

"So what are two nice girls like you doing in a place like this?" Jim asked. He laughed at his own attempt at humor, causing the blubbery folds under his weak chin to jiggle like meat-flavored jello.

"We're waiting for a handsome captain," I quipped.

"Yes! That's what we're doing," Cold Cuts said, and laughed with relief.

"Well, aren't you lucky, then," Jim said, eyeing Cold Cuts lasciviously. He grinned, exposing an off-colored front tooth. "You know, I just happen to be a captain myself."

"Are you now?" I said.

"Yes, I am." Suddenly, Jim's face looked pained, as if he'd been stabbed with a fork. "Um...excuse me ladies. Nature calls." He heaved himself off the barstool and waddled toward the men's room.

"You don't think he's our sailboat captain, do you?" Cold Cuts asked.

The thought made my stomach turn. "If he is, I'm gonna sue the place for false advertising. Come on. Let's get out of here before he comes back." I took a step toward the beach.

"Wait," Cold Cuts grabbed my arm. "We've still got twenty minutes before we're supposed to meet at the boat. Don't you want a drink first?"

"If you think a drink's gonna make *that* guy look better, you're out of your mind!"

"Come on. What's the harm?" Cold Cuts turned to the bartender. "Two margaritas, please. Put them on my tab." She shot me a devilish grin.

"I don't trust that look. What are you up to?"

"I just gotta know," Cold Cuts confessed.

"Know what?"

Cold Cuts bent over and whispered in my ear. "If that thing on his head is real. Come on. Aren't you curious?"

I pulled back. "Aww, geeze!"

Cold Cuts batted her big brown eyes and patted the barstool next to her. "Come on. It'll be fun. I mean, what else have we got to do?"

"But...how –"

"I'll distract him," Cold Cuts explained, cutting me off. "Then you sneak up behind him and get a good look. Shhh! He's coming back."

I sat and watched as Jim waddled toward us like an orange Shamu Slushie. Cold Cuts smiled at him coyly and winked. "What took you so long, handsome?"

Jim almost managed to hide his surprise at the compliment. "What? Oh! Did you miss me?" he said, and smiled in a way that made me want to go bleach something.

"Of course!" Cold Cuts said, and practically shoved me off my barstool. "My friend needs to use the facilities, too. Where were they?"

Jim hitched a greasy pink thumb over his sloping shoulder. "Back that-a-way."

I got up and took about ten steps in that general direction, then turned around and shrugged at Cold Cuts. She winked and motioned for me to come up behind him. She grabbed Jim's Spam hand and got busy chatting him up like a professional flirt. He fell for it, hook line and sinker.

Now all I had to do was figure out if he was fishing with real or artificial bait.

Cold Cuts kept the tub of gelatinous man-flesh busy while I snuck up on him from behind. Perched on a barstool, he was taller than I'd expected. I teetered on my tiptoes about a foot behind him and peered at the shabby, gray mat of fur clinging to his noggin. I still couldn't tell for sure, so I tried to part it at the scalp with a toothpick I found lying on the bar. I stuck the pick into the swirl of hair at the back of his head....

"Your margaritas, ladies," the bartender said, startling me like a priest caught at a peep show.

"Whaaaa—!" I lost my balance on my tiptoes, wind-milled my arms wildly, and fell, face forward onto Jim's huge, orange back. The impact knocked Jim over. He fell to his knees onto the sand floor. The toothpick jutting from his hair snagged on the hem of Cold Cuts' sundress and yanked Jim's toupee clean off his liver-spotted head.

"Ack! Ack!" Jim gurgled and clutched at his throat as he hit the sand.

Too mortified to move, before I could register what was happening, the bartender ran around the counter and encircled Jim in his arms.

He tried to perform the Heimlich on him, but the young man's arms couldn't stretch all the way around Jim's substantial midriff. The bartender gave up, circled around Jim on his knees and punched him in the gut. A martini olive shot out of Jim's mouth and ricocheted across the cabana bar like a slimy ping-pong ball.

"Oh my lord! I'm so sorry!" I said.

Jim sucked in a lungful of air and shot me a dirty look. Then he felt the top of his head and immediately started grabbing at the sandy ground around him.

"Sir!" the bartender said, "You need to remain calm!"

"Need...my...." Jim gasped.

Cold Cuts grabbed his toupee, shook the sand off it and offered it to Jim. He snatched it out of her hand and slapped it on top of his head.

"I think you've got it on backwards," Cold Cuts said, then bit her lip hard.

"Why, you two ingrates!" Jim screeched.

"We were only –' Cold Cuts began.

"I think you should leave," the bartender interrupted. "Just go. Let him cool off."

"We're sorry. Let us know if there's anything we can do," I said to Jim.

His blubbery face was almost the color of his shirt. He shot me a look so deadly, that even if I'd been a cat, all my lives would have been used up.

"Thank you," said the bartender, glancing from Jim to me. "But as you can see, I think you've already done enough."

Chapter Ten

Cold Cuts and I slunk away from the cabana bar like a pair of hapless felons, leaving Jim to recover from his close brush with the grim reaper's martini. The way I saw it, it wasn't choking on an olive that had nearly done Jim in. If we hadn't left when we did, I think the poor guy would have died of embarrassment.

"Hurry up!" Cold Cuts called.

We'd been following the shoreline toward the sailboat, and she'd run along ahead of me. The unexpected turn our toupee investigation had taken left us running short of time. If we were going to catch the sunset sail promised by Monty and his glossy brochure, we had to hoof it down the beach – and fast.

The sailboat finally came into view, and I grabbed Cold Cuts by the arm, my chest heaving. "Slow down! Let me catch my breath!"

Cold Cuts stopped and laughed. "Well, that was a pretty hair raising affair," she joked.

"Cold Cuts! Are you *nuts?* How did I ever let you talk me into doing that?"

"Hey," Cold Cuts teased, "you're the one who ripped his wig off. I just wanted an opinion – not a look under the hood. All *I* did was chat you up to him."

"But it was *your* idea! Hey, wait a second. What do you mean, chat *me* up?"

"Come on. Jim's just a lonely old guy. You know he's *way* too old for *me*."

Indignity straightened my spinal column. "But not for *me?*"

Cold Cuts rolled her big, brown eyes. "Okay. For *both* of us. I mean, he's too old for my *granny*. Besides, I told him you were already spoken for, so you're off the hook."

Cold Cuts began walking toward the boat. I tagged along behind her, my feet twisting in the sugary sand.

"What do you mean? Why did you tell him I was spoken for?" I called out behind her.

She twisted her torso to face me, but kept trudging along, her blue dress flapping in the evening sea breeze. "Because you *are*. Or did I get that wrong?"

"I'm not joined at the hip with Tom," I heard myself argue. "I mean, it's not like we're married. We're *barely* engaged."

"Uh oh. Do I smell trouble in paradise?"

I scowled. The sun was setting over the ocean and the sky was gorgeous, but all I could see was red. "No. That's not what I'm saying. You told that guy Jim that I was spoken for. That makes me feel, I dunno, like somehow the fun part of my life is over."

Cold Cuts stopped and let me catch up with her again. "Wow. That's not good, Val. But you know, Tom's not to blame for the way you feel."

"Who's blaming Tom?" I said angrily.

"You are."

"Me? I *am not!*"

"Aren't you? Think about it. Did Tom force you to take that engagement ring?"

"No."

"Has he forbidden you to see your friends, or to ever have fun again?"

"No," I pouted.

"Well then, who *did?*"

"I...uh –"

"Well if it isn't my favorite pair – Drunk and Disorderly," a voice boomed out across the water from the vicinity of the sailboat.

Cold Cuts looked over and laughed. I didn't. Our so-called handsome sea captain turned out to be Bill Robo, the man-bun model. "Welcome aboard, ladies," he called from the bow.

"Well, this ought to be fun," I muttered, and stuck a toe into the mild surf. The water was tepid. Not warm, but warmer than I'd expected for April.

"You coming?" Cold Cuts asked. Water was already up to her shins and she was halfway to the boat. I followed suit and waded, knee deep, into the Gulf. When we reached the side of the sailboat, Guru Bill hauled both of us up, in turn, with surprising strength and dexterity.

"Looks like you two are my entire crew tonight," he said. "We'll be taking an hour-long sail to Dog Island and back. Sit back and get comfy." As we settled into the cushioned seats at the front of the boat, Bill added, "Oh yeah. Safety preliminaries. Your life vests are located under your seats. And I presume you read the brochure and left all your valuables, cell phones and personal electronics in your rooms?"

"*Personal electronics?*" I asked.

"Yes. Headsets, cameras, exercise monitors," Bill explained. He looked at me and winked. "Why? What were *you* thinking?"

I forced a smile and silently stewed over whether that joke was part of Bill's regular tourist routine, or if he'd invented it just for me. I couldn't tell. *Dang. Man Bun's pretty slick.*

"Any other questions?" Bill asked and shot me a mischievous grin.

"Will we have time for a swim?" Cold Cuts asked. "We're wearing bikinis."

"Well, in that case," Bill said with a devilish smile, "I'll see to it that you get the chance."

"Cool," Cold Cuts said, and relaxed into the cushions beside me.

The evening sky was a rainbow of pink and purple as Bill hoisted up the anchor and worked the mainsail. Soon we were cruising comfortably toward a small speck of land backlit against the horizon. Salt spray freshened the air, and I finally let go and relaxed into the moment. I closed my eyes and took in a deep breath as the cool, evening breeze swept my hair from my face and my troubles from my mind....

Then something splattered against my closed eyelid.

My eyes flew open. I wiped my eye. It was only water. I looked over at Cold Cuts. She was staring dreamily out to sea. Bill, in turn, was staring at Cold Cuts. I shook my head and closed my eyes again. Another drop of water hit me. Then another. I opened my eyes just in time to see lightening flash in the distance.

"Uh oh," Bill said.

"What do you mean, 'uh oh'?" I asked.

"Looks like a thunderstorm brewing," Bill said. "And it's coming up fast."

Another lightning bolt streaked across the sky. Cold Cuts grumbled, "I hate lightening."

"We need to take cover," I said.

"Absolutely," Bill agreed. "We don't have time to waste. We're closer to Dog Island than the shore. We'll have to wait it out there."

"But –" I started to protest, but our captain wasn't listening.

Like a wild chimp on a clothesline, Bill sprang up and started fooling around with sails and booms and whatever all those ropes and things on a sailboat are called. The wind started blowing in short gusts, and the boat began to wobble. Cold Cuts and I held onto each other as the sky drew darker and the rain grew heavier.

"It's okay, ladies," Bill's voice called from somewhere above us in the swirling darkness. Each lightning strike delivered a quick glimpse of man-bun Bill scurrying about here and there. I was beginning to feel as if I were trapped in soggy disco flashback when, finally, the boat's bottom hit something. The impact caused me and Cold Cuts to lurch forward, nearly out of our seats.

"After me," Bill's voice sounded. In a flash of lightning, I saw him jump out of the boat.

"Wait for us!" I screamed as he disappeared in the darkness.

"I'm here," he called. "Jump."

"Let's go!" I said, and tugged Cold Cuts to standing. "Jump with me."

"Hurry!" Bill's voice sounded nearby.

I flung myself into the water, in the direction of Bill's voice. He caught me by the arm, keeping my head from going underwater. Once I was steady on my feet, he pushed me toward the shore. "Go!" he shouted.

"My friend!" I said.

"Go," he commanded again, "before she jumps on your head. I've got her."

Slightly stunned, I did as I was told.

"Okay," he called to Cold Cuts. "Jump!"

I heard her shriek behind me, then splash into the water. I was nearly to shore when Bill breezed by me, holding Cold Cuts in his arms like a hero in a romance novel. Prince charming carried his elegant princess to shore, while I waded behind them like a sodden old lady's maid. A streak of lightening illuminated the scene as he lay her gently on the sand.

"You okay?" he asked.

"Yes, I am," Cold Cuts answered.

"Me too," I said.

"Good," Bill said. "Follow me."

Chapter Eleven

So much for a luxury honeymoon suite at a fancy resort. Shivering and soaked to the bone, Cold Cuts and I were holed up in the storm with Jesus' twin brother in a driftwood lean-to covered by an old tarp with more holes in it than a moth-ridden slice of Swiss cheese. Rain poured in tiny rivulets through the holes and onto our heads as we sat in wet sand and cringed at the lightning show all around us. Like an old-timey flash bulb, each blue-white strike delivered a millisecond glimpse of the sailboat bobbing eerily offshore like a mysterious sea monster.

"We can't go anywhere until the lightning lets up," Bill said. "I suggest you pull your dresses over your heads and bury your legs in the dirt."

"What?" Cold Cuts and I protested.

I looked at him, wild-eyed. "You're not gonna murderize us, are you?"

"What?" Bill asked. "No! But if you don't do like I say, the bugs might."

A mosquito buzzed around my nose. "Oh, crap."

As if summoned by his words, a horde of mosquitoes and no-see-ums descended on us like a Biblical plague. I started swatting and slapping and scratching like a nudist lost in the Everglades. A flash of lightning illuminated an old tin can in the sand next to me. I grabbed it and started digging. Cold Cuts found a kid's plastic beach shovel. Globs of wet sand began flying around the driftwood lean-to like sodden popcorn in a microwave bag.

"I think that'll do it, ladies," Bill said, wiping sand from his face. "Now, lay on your stomachs and pull your dresses up over your heads. I'll cover your legs with sand."

Cold Cuts and I exchanged glances and nods, then obeyed his commands. We lay down in the shallow trenches we'd dug and Bill heaped cool, wet sand onto our flea-bitten flesh. The skirts of our dresses formed makeshift tents around our arms and faces. Once he'd covered us, Bill squeezed into the narrow space between us and covered his own feet and legs as best he could. Then he lay down and stuck his hairy head inside a crumpled potato chip bag.

"I hope this isn't on video," I said into the grey darkness.

Bill burst out laughing. His chip bag puffed with air. The wind caught it and nearly blew it away before he grabbed it and repositioned in on his face. The utter absurdity of our situation suddenly overwhelmed me. I exploded with laughter. Cold Cuts joined in, followed by Bill. The three of us laughed until we were spent. Then we snuggled a little closer together and waited quietly in the dark as our little hobo tent on Dog Island swayed precariously in the storm.

I WOKE TO THE SOUND of someone whispering beside me. I licked at the sand on my lips and started to answer, then I realized the voice wasn't speaking to me.

"The dog lover's only after one thing," Bill's husky voice whispered into the night.

"What's that?" Cold Cuts asked.

"Availability," Bill answered. "The dog lover operates on pure lust. He has sex with a girl, pulls up his pants, and starts sniffing around for the next one."

Oh great. Our yoga guru/sea captain is also a love expert. This ought to be entertaining.

"Then there's the lizard lover," man-bun continued. "He's always on the lookout for 'the one,' but he's never satisfied. He chooses a woman, but he doesn't stay long enough to build a real connection. He may help her dig a nest, but then he disappears, leaving her to fend for herself."

I must be delirious. This is kind of making sense....

"But then there's the monkey lover," Bill whispered.

"What's so great about the monkey lover?" Cold Cuts asked.

"He takes his time. He knows what he wants. He chooses his lover wisely, according to the attributes he desires in a mate. The monkey lover romances his girl."

"How?" Cold Cuts asked.

"He shares his food. He grooms her. He fends off her enemies. He's devoted to her alone. He protects her and her family."

Oh, give me a break. This guy's a sleaze. Either that, or I'm way too jaded about love.

I opened my mouth to speak, but was stopped short by a low moan. The storm had passed, and in the dappled moonlight shining through the holes in the tarp, I made out a slight movement. Bill was leaning over Cold Cuts, kissing her. She didn't seem to be minding. In fact, just the opposite.

I suddenly felt as old and out of place as a deaf grandma at a heavy metal rave. I froze in place. *Should I say something, or keep quiet?*

Bill climbed on top of Cold Cuts. I cringed as something landed on the skirt-tent covering my face. It looked like a bikini bottom.

I'm already in too deep to speak up now. I scrunched my eyes closed and tried to focus on the sound of the breeze and the waves.

I guess they don't call this "Dog" Island for nothing.

I WOKE TO FIND OUR yoga guru, sailboat captain and guest "services" expert with his hand on me, shaking me by the shoulder. I could barely believe it. I'd dozed off during his shenanigans with Cold Cuts! *Geeze. I really* must *be getting old.*

"What do you want?" I hissed.

"Hey. Take it easy. The storm's over. We can sail back now."

"What time is it?"

"Who cares?" Cold Cuts said huskily.

I rolled onto and elbow and sat up. "You're right. Let's get out of this place."

We abandoned our hobo hut and sailed back toward the glow of scattered lights on the mainland. A dip in the cool Gulf before we boarded had washed most of the sand from our bodies, but had left us chilled to the bone. Bill found some blankets in the berth and wrapped us both up tight. As for himself, he seemed content in his soggy linen pants and shirt. Maybe all that afterglow was keeping him warm....

As we anchored offshore in front of the resort, I studied Bill in the misty moonlight.

"Thanks for getting us home safe," I said. "That was certainly an adventure."

"Yeah. One for the bucket list," Cold Cuts said, and shot him a wink.

Bill anchored the boat and flung out a ladder. The three of us climbed over and waded to shore. Cold Cuts stayed close to Bill, so I decided to give the two lovebirds a moment alone.

"I'm gonna go get the room key," I said. "Meet you back at cottage 22."

"What if it's not ready?" Cold Cuts asked.

"Then you should be able to hear me scream from there."

The three of us shared a brief laugh. The inky sky was calm and still and perfect. *Romantic*, even. The surf was calm, as if the storm had never happened.

"Okay, then. I'm off," I said, and strolled toward the lights of the resort, dreaming I was thirty-something again.

AS I PICKED MY WAY along the path in the direction of the hotel lobby, it dawned on me that I was alone. Outside. At night. In a strange place. A chill straightened my spine.

The tropical plants that had seemed so colorful and friendly along the trail during the day suddenly took on a sinister tone. The hair on my scalp stood up, and my feet picked up the pace. I was about halfway down the path when a movement in the bushes nearly startled the piss out of me. I opened my mouth to scream, but then I saw the cause of the commotion, and nearly laughed with relief instead.

Sticking out of the palm fronds was the beekeeper's hat of that fishing weirdo Cold Cuts and I had run into earlier. When I reached out to grab it, I realized it was occupied. *That's* when I screamed.

"Arrghh!"

"Hard-bodied grubs," the head in the bushes said.

"What are you *doing?* You nearly scared me to –"

A flashlight clicked on and shot into my eyes like a laser beam from a UFO. My hands flew up to protect my eyes. "Geeze!" I shrieked. "What's your problem?"

The head didn't answer, but the flashlight cut out. Between white spots burned into my retinas, I watched as the head in the bushes rose to about six feet off the ground. The body it was attached to turned around and disappeared between a patch of croton bushes.

I stumbled, half-blind, down the path until the lights of the lobby came into view. I marched through the doors looking like a startled, half-drown, flea-bitten rodent.

"Good evening," Monty said without even so much as a second glance. He reached over the desk and slid something across the counter toward me.

"Your room keys, Ms. Fremden. Your 'luggage' is already in your room."

Chapter Twelve

I woke up clean, dry, and safe from being drowned or electrocuted by Mother Nature.

Now this is more like it!

I stretched my arms and legs out amongst the pile of fluffy pillows in my deliciously comfy bed. I stared up at the thatched ceiling. No raindrops landed in my eyes.

A cute, grunting noise made me glance to my right. Cold Cuts was sawing logs in the queen bed beside mine. The clock on the nightstand read 5:03 a.m.

I smiled with contentment – and also a trace of envy. *I wish I could sleep in like that.* But it was becoming clear that turning fifty and waking up at 5 a.m. came as a matched set. Back in December, after my *real* birthday, middle-age and early rising had shown up on my doorstop, stuck together like conjoined twins. Neither could escape the other, and now *I* couldn't escape them.

My bladder pinged warnings it was ready to burst. I sighed and lifted the covers carefully, so as not to make a noise. I sidled to the edge of the bed and slowly crept out, then tiptoed across the room to the bathroom.

Surrounded by the luxury amenities of the cottage, the whole episode last night with the storm seemed like a bad dream. But one look in the vanity mirror convinced me it had been real enough. My thighs and butt cheeks were peppered with small, red blotches. As soon as I saw them, the bites began to itch.

"Arrgghh!"

I curled my fingers into fists and forced myself not to scratch. I did my business, then crept back into the bedroom. Cold Cuts was still asleep. I picked silently through my open suitcase. I'd packed for a romantic getaway, so I didn't have any comfort clothes with me. I slipped into a fresh sundress and a light sweater. Then I grabbed my purse and I sneaked out the door.

Our tiny thatched-roof cottage looked darling in the soft, morning twilight. I hung a "Do Not Disturb" sign on the knob, then went in search of the nectar of life – a strong cup of coffee.

WHEN IT CAME TO COFFEE, Tom told me I had the nose of a bloodhound. Maybe he was right. I caught the scent in the salty air and followed it along the sandy path to the lobby. No one was at the desk, but the blessed smell of coffee filled the space. I sniffed my way to a small breakfast room where a large, silver thermos of hot java was already perked and waiting on a table next to paper cups and white, china mugs.

I snatched a paper cup from the columnar stack, filled it with coffee, milk and two sugars and drank it down like a drunk on a weekend bender. I fixed myself another cup and fitted a plastic lid on top. Satiated for the moment, I glanced around the room. Small rattan tables for two lined the walls. A bookshelf by the door offered an informal place for visitors to exchange paperbacks. I sipped my second cup of coffee and read through the titles.

Lost in Paradise caught my eye. I took the novel from the lending library, then sneaked out of the lobby and back down the tropical path to the shore. I laid my things on one of the resort's fancy blue beach loungers. A pair of crisp, white beach towels were already laid across the back of the cozy chaise built for two. I looked around for the resort staff, but for the moment, it appeared I had the beach to myself. I laid the book down to claim my spot, then went for a short stroll along the shore in the early morning mist.

I WHILED AWAY THE MORNING sunning, reading and napping. The hapless girl in *Lost in Paradise* was waving in vain at another distant rescue boat when my cellphone rang. It was Tom, and it was precisely 8:30 a.m.

"Hey. How are things going?" he teased, his voice upbeat.

"Good. How about you?"

"I tried calling last night. You didn't answer."

"Oh. I'm sorry. I didn't realize it. Cold Cuts and I went sailing. We couldn't take our phones with us."

"That sounds like fun. Sorry I missed it."

"Don't be. We had a...well, *adventurous* evening."

Tom's cheerful voice dialed down a notch. "Uh oh. What does *that* mean?"

"Nothing to worry about. We're fine. In fact, I'm lying in a lounger right now, watching the world go by."

"Don't let it go by without me."

"I won't. How's Jorge doing with his exams?"

"Too soon to tell. I just left him at the academy. He's taking them now."

"Does he seem, you know, prepared?"

Tom sighed. "Well, he's still alive. That counts for something."

"Is he really that bad off, Tom? Maybe he shouldn't push himself so hard."

"He's got to start somewhere, Val. He's nervous, yeah. I mean, who wouldn't be? But I think he can do it."

"I hope you're right. When will he know the results?"

"Not until the end of the week. Until then, Goober and Winky will have to hold him together. I want to be here when Jorge gets done around noon today. I'm gonna take him to lunch, then I should be able to leave here around 2 p.m."

"Good. Tell him I wish him the best, okay?"

"Will do."

I glanced around the beach. Tourist traffic had picked up, but none of the sun-seekers were looking my way. I scratched a couple of bites on my butt. "Can you bring my chamomile lotion with you?"

"Sure."

"Oh. And my white bathing suit? I seem to have forgotten it."

"It's already packed."

"Aha! So you *did* sabotage me."

"Hey. Can't a fellow enjoy seeing his fiancée in a gold thong bikini?"

"Well, you probably won't like what you see – especially now."

"Why? What's happened?"

"Like I said, nothing life-threatening."

"That's all the explanation I get?"

"Hey, I have to lure you here with *something*, don't I?"

"I'd say you're already fishing with the right bait. See you around 3 p.m."

"Okay. Bye."

"Oh," Tom said, his voice a little flat. "In case you were worried, Winky was able to salvage your ring from the garbage disposal."

"Oh," I said, my face suddenly hot. "That's great!"

"I'll bring it with me."

"Super!" I said way too enthusiastically. I clicked off the phone and felt like a turd. *Was I a bad fiancé?* My stomach answered with a gurgle. I sat up in the lounger and lay my novel aside. *Maybe breakfast would make me a better fiancé.*

I STOPPED BY OUR LITTLE thatched cottage on the way to the breakfast room. The "Do Not Disturb" sign was still hanging on the knob. I slid my key into the lock and peeked inside. Cold Cuts was still in a heap of covers in bed. It appeared that, this morning at least, I'd be having breakfast alone.

Monty was at his post at the reception desk when I strolled into the lobby. "Good morning, miss," he said in his snooty British accent.

"Good morning. Just going to breakfast."

"Will your companion be joining you?" he asked.

"Uh...not this morning."

Monty's left eyebrow ticked up a hair. "Very good, miss. Follow me."

Even though I knew the way, I let Monty lead me to the breakfast room. The cozy little nook was empty except for one other person. I recognized the backside of his unmistakable toupee and froze in my tracks.

"Uh...you know what," I whispered to Monty. "I forgot something. I'll come back later."

Monty eyed me suspiciously. "As you wish, miss."

I shot him a sheepish, fake smile, then turned and walked as fast as I could toward the lobby exit. When I stepped outside into the open, salty air, I sighed with relief. I'd escaped unnoticed by Jim. My stomach growled again, reminding me I was hungrier than a toothless termite in a pile of sawdust. Earlier, when I'd been lying on the lounger at the beach, I'd smelled coffee wafting upwind from the south. Maybe there was a breakfast place that banned bad toupees....

The tropical jungle maze between the reception building and the beach had become familiar territory. I wound my way through it with ease. When I got to the place I'd seen the old guy in the beekeeper's hat, I hesitated. I'd meant to ask Monty about him, but the sight of Jim's awful toupee hanging precariously over the waffle machine had rocketed the thought clear out of my head. I looked around, but there was no sign of the fishing hat or the weirdo it belonged to. I shrugged and continued my way toward the beach.

When I stepped out of the tropical maze, a gust of wind caught my skirt and nearly blew it over my head.

"It's a breezy one today!" Brad, the hunky porter said. The sight of him in nothing but a pair of shorts and a tank top made me forget all about the weather. "Nice day for a stroll," he added.

"Yes, it is," I answered, pressing my skirt to my thighs with my palms. "Any place to grab breakfast around here?"

"Our breakfast room should be open now."

"Yes. It is. But I was looking for something...uh...with more *local* flavor?"

Brad flashed me his diamond smile. "Sure. Try Doug's Dugout. It's just before the pink building down there." Brad pointed to a spot about a quarter mile south down the sandy, white beach. "They have the best Mahi breakfast burritos around."

"Thanks," I said, then wondered if there was such an abundance of restaurants offering Mahi breakfast burritos that Brad could make that comparison. *Does it really matter?* I asked myself. *Not a flip,* I answered. So, I nodded and smiled at the handsome blond cabana boy, then set my sights on the shoreline and the pink spot down the beach.

Instead of padding along in the sand, I shuffled my way, shin deep, in the gentle surf that broke just a few feet from shore. The rhythmic motion of the waves carved a small, underwater ditch in the sand parallel to the shore. Over the years, I'd learned that's where the best shells collected. As I waded along the trough line, I wondered how many untold hours I'd spent mesmerized by the shifting water, waiting with anticipation at what the next wave would reveal....

"Got 'cha!" I said, and plucked a sleek, smooth olive shell from the foamy, foot-deep water. The size and shape of a date, the shell was a pale, grey-green color and as shiny as glass. No sooner had I grabbed it when I spotted another. By the time I was halfway to Doug's Dugout, my hands were full of olive shells, cat's paws, angel wings and a nice-sized shark-eye.

I was about to call it a day and head to breakfast when I saw it. It rolled over my toes, and came into view through a sheet of clear water formed as a wave pulled back. It was a rare *Junonia Florida*. Spotted like a giraffe, it was one of a handful of elusive shells I'd been searching for my whole life. And this one looked like a perfect specimen.

I reached down for it and suddenly the world turned upside down. I tumbled into the surf, my shells raining into the sea like scattered hail. Someone had slammed into me.

"I so sorry!" the man said in a heavy, Spanish accent.

"Watch where you're going!" I yelled, floundering in the surf.

He grabbed my arm and pulled me to standing. His eyes were wild. "You!" he yelled in my face. "You get out here! Now!"

"Get away from me!" I hissed and yanked my arm away.

"Mira!" he yelled, and pointed to the sky behind me. "Mira! Mira!"

I turned around. Not far off, the sky had turned a funny shade of light purple, yellow and brown, like a half-healed bruise. In the middle of it, stretching down like a witch's finger, a funnel cloud poked its way down toward the surface of the Gulf.

"Holy crap!" I cried.

"Jes! Holly chit!" The man repeated, and ran off in the direction of Doug's Dugout.

I blinked, disbelieving. It was like something out of a bad movie. I stood, open mouthed, as the water spout took aim for the shoreline. It looked to be about the same distance from the Sunset Sail-Away Resort as I was, but on the opposite end of the beach. I thought about the little thatched hut Cold Cuts and I were staying in.

That place can't withstand a direct hit! I have to warn her!

A sudden gust of wind swirled sand in my eyes. I steeled myself and ran headlong back toward the resort.

THE BOAT WE'D SAILED in last night was bobbing madly in the water as I ran past it. The stinging sand blasted away at my arms and legs as I stumbled up to the head of the tropical trail like Dorothy at the gate in *The Wizard of Oz*. The foliage and bushes whipped wildly back and forth, and I turned back for a last look. The blasted tornado from hell was headed right for me! I screeched, took a step forward, and fell face-first onto the wind-eroded remains of a tourist's sandcastle. I'd stepped in the hole excavated in the sand beside it.

This can't be happening!

I scrambled to my feet. My left ankle hurt like mad as I hobbled my way down the path to the little wooden sign marked, "Cottage 22." Through a swirl of leaves and sand and garbage set free from the beach trash bins, I could barely make out the thatched hut I shared with Cold Cuts. I fiddled with key as the tornado barreled down toward me.

Open! Open! Open, would you?

Finally, the key gave way. The door flew open as if hit by a Mack truck.

"Cold Cuts, take cover!" I screamed, and ran to her bed. I rifled through the mound of pillows, but she wasn't there. Suddenly, the bed covers lifted up in the air as if possessed by demons. The lamp started wobbling its way off the nightstand.

The door! I need to close the door!

I took a step and yelped with pain. I grabbed the bedpost for support, then hobbled toward the door. Everything that wasn't nailed down was spinning around the room like a snow globe gone mad. A bra flapped into my face. I peeled it away, grabbed the door knob and pushed. But the force of the wind was too much for me on one foot. I gave up and stared out at the swirling, grey-green sky, until a foot came flying toward my face and everything went pitch black.

Chapter Thirteen

I dreamed I was swirling in a vortex, holding on for dear life to a white bird the size of a rabbit. It struggled in my arms, trying to get free. "Let go," it screeched over and over. "Let go! Let go!"

The sharp cry of a seagull stirred me to consciousness. I cracked open a wary eye. I was lying on my side on the floor of the thatched cottage, facing the wide-open front entryway. A large, white bird took a tentative, pigeon-toed step toward me on its clownish, yellow feet. From my perspective on the floor, it looked huge and menacing.

"Shoo!" I coughed, and flailed my free arm at it. It screeched, hopped twice and flew out the door. Only then did I realize I was hugging someone's detached leg like a teddy bear.

"Aaarghh!"

I shoved the horrid leg away from me. It tumbled halfway across the room and came to rest with a light, hollow thud on the buff-colored tile. I nearly fainted with relief. It was plastic. Somewhere in town, a manikin was in need of ambulatory assistance.

I sat up and looked around. The room was an absolute shambles. I'd left my suitcase open, and, apparently, Cold Cuts had neglected to secure her grocery bags. The tornado had blown our crap to kingdom come. Either that, or Cold Cuts was getting ready to hold the most poorly organized yard sale in the history of mankind. The thought of her caused my groggy mind to snap to attention.

"Cold Cuts!" I yelled. "Where are you?"

There was no reply.

I tried to struggle to my feet, but the pain radiating from my swollen ankle nixed that plan. I crawled over a jumble of bras and toothbrushes and flip flops toward the phone on the nightstand. I tugged at the machine, but it held tight, fastened to the table with screws. I pulled myself up to lean with my back against the bed and grabbed for the receiver. I was surprised, and relieved, to discover there was actually a dial tone.

I punched zero for reception. Monty picked up.

"Thank you for calling Sunset Sail-Away Beach Resort, where all your holiday dreams –"

"Monty!" I cut in. "It's Val Fremden in hut 22."

"You mean *cottage* 22, miss?"

"Whatever! Listen, there was a tornado. There's a leg in my room. I can't walk. Please send help!"

"My word, madam. Have you lost a leg?"

"No! There's just a leg in my…Look. I can't walk because –"

"You've been drinking?"

"What? No! Didn't you see the tornado?"

"No. Not personally. But I heard there's been one."

"Well, it nearly blew me away! I fell and twisted my ankle. I need help."

"I see. Very good, miss. I'll send our first-aid squad right away."

"Thanks."

I hung up the receiver and waited, feeling like just another piece of broken garbage amongst the heap of rubble in the room. A glint of movement above my head caught my eye. It was the bottom of my thong bikini. The scrap of shiny, gold material was snagged on the ornate frame of an expensive-looking portrait of the resort's founder. I'd noticed the painting of "Sir William F. Rockbottom, III" late last night, when I'd finally been able to check into the room.

I giggled despite the pain in my ankle. Mother Nature sure had a weird sense of humor. To think, my bikini bottom now dangled lewdly over the man's smug, aristocratic face.

Take that, mister high and mighty!

"Ms. Fremden?"

The voice belonged to Monty. "Yes. I'm here!" I called out from behind the bed.

Monty stepped into view. Against the ruined room, he appeared as neat and clean and out of place as a butler in a landfill. "Oh my. What happened?" he asked in his understated, British way.

"I told you. A tornado."

"Yes, I can see that," he said. He snatched the bikini bottom from Sir Rockbottom's face. "I thought you were joking."

"I wish I was."

"Right. Um...I'm sorry for the delay. I couldn't locate our first-aid squad. I've already notified EMS. They should be here any moment."

"Thanks, Monty. Listen, have you seen my friend?"

"Miss Foreman? No. Not since yesterday," Monty answered. "One moment, please." He disappeared out the door. I heard him talking on the phone. "Yes...um...we need an ambulance. Yes. No. Okay."

Really, Monty? You're gonna lie about having called EMS?

Monty reappeared, his face more pinched than usual. "May I bring you anything miss, while you're awaiting the...ambulance?"

"A Tanqueray and tonic wouldn't hurt."

Monty appeared a bit startled, perhaps uncertain whether I was joking or not. That made two of us. "Very good, miss," he said, and disappeared again.

BY THE TIME THE TWO EMS techs arrived, I'd managed to drag my fat butt to where I had a view of the front door. When they stepped inside, I forgot all about my ankle. The two young men could have starred in a calendar for Sexy Techs of Sarasota.

"Wow," said the blond one. "Looks like you had a barroom brawl in here."

"Thanks. I like to do my own decorating," I sneered.

"Glad to see you haven't lost your sense of humor," he said, and knelt beside me. "Let me take a look at that ankle."

"Anyone else in here?" his buff, brunette colleague asked.

"No," I answered. "I'm here with a friend, but I haven't been able to find her."

"Looks like a sprain," the first EMT said. "Does this hurt?" He turned my ankle slightly and a blue volt of electricity seared my brain.

"Owwww!" I cried. "Compared to what? Being trampled by an elephant?"

"Sorry about that," he said. "But the good news is, it's not broken. Just a sprain. I'll wrap it up. You'll need to stay off it for a few days."

"Count yourself lucky," said second EMT joked, and held up the manikin leg. "You're still better off than this gal."

"Thankfully, that twister only tore through a small block of town," said the blond as he wound a bandage around my ankle. "I bet that leg belongs to Betty's Bargain Barn. Mind if I take it to her?"

"Knock yourself out," I said. "I already did."

The two men chuckled. "You're a real joker," the handsome brunette said. "Hey, I hate to ask, but do you mind if I use your restroom?"

"No. That's fine. Hopefully maid service will be here soon to clean the place up. There's no telling what it looks like in there."

"No worries," he said, and stepped over the rubble toward the bathroom behind me.

"That ought to do it," said the blond EMT. He fastened a metal pin on the bandage around my ankle and stood up. "Stay here. I'm going to get you a wheelchair."

"Uh, Charlie?" the brunette called to his friend. "You better come take a look at this."

Charlie walked over to the bathroom and whistled long and low.

"Whatever's in there, you have to blame on the tornado, not me!" I joked. But neither man laughed.

"Better call homicide," I heard Charlie say.

"What?" I asked.

The demeanor of both EMTs switched from warm to frigid like the faucets on a tap. They whispered something to each other behind my back.

"What's in the bathroom?" I asked again.

"Take it easy ma'am," Charlie said, his friendly tone nowhere to be heard. "You need to remain calm. We'll get you into a wheelchair."

"I'll make the call," the brunette said, and shot me a disgusted look as he disappeared out the door.

"Listen, Charlie," I said to the EMT. "I need to find my friend."

"Lady," Charlie hissed. "You're not going anywhere."

Chapter Fourteen

My legs stuck out sideways from the wheelchair as I leaned over and strained to see inside the window of our cottage. I'd been rolled unceremoniously onto the front porch by the EMS guys and left to wait outside for an officer of the law to arrive. The blond EMT had locked the chair's wheels before he left, and warned me to stay put. With my foot throbbing like a recently hammered thumb, it wasn't like I had much choice. I leaned over and squinted into the glass, but the glare of the sun turned the panes to mirrors, and I couldn't make out diddly squat inside.

"Val Fremden?" a man's voice sounded, catching me off guard.

I turned around and my stomach fell to my knees. It was Jim. From the bar. Bad toupee and all.

"Oh, it's *you*," he said. His already cold eyes hardened to frozen steel.

"Um...yes. Hi, there. You've got to help me. What's going on, Jim?"

"The name's *Detective James Stanley*, Sarasota Homicide Division," he corrected me harshly. "And that's what I'm here to find out."

"Homicide division? But...I just have a sprained ankle."

"Right," Detective Stanley barked. I watched, dumbfounded, as he pulled a pair of light-blue, shower-cap looking things from a briefcase and stretched them over his shoes. He opened the door to the cottage, entered, and closed the door behind him. A bad feeling began to boil in my gut. He came back out a minute or so later, shaking his head and glaring at me.

"Tell me, Ms. Fremden. Are you alone?"

"Yes, but..."

"So, why are both beds unmade?"

"I thought you meant right *now*. A friend – the one you met last night – she spent the night."

"Hmmph," he grunted condescendingly. "There appears to be signs of a struggle inside. Did you two have an argument?"

"No. All that mess is because of the tornado."

"I see. So, then, where is this 'friend' of yours now?"

"I don't know. I went for a walk on the beach. Then the tornado came up. It chased me all the way back to the room. Then I got hit in the head with the leg and –"

"What leg?"

"The plastic manikin leg."

"I didn't see any leg."

"What?" I fell into confusion for a moment. "Oh. I forgot. One of the EMTs took it. It belonged to his friend Betsy or something like that."

Detective Stanley eyed me dubiously. "Uh huh. Well, your head looks fine to me. Tell me, Ms. Fremden, are you on drugs of any kind?"

"No...."

"The EMTs said you were laughing and joking, and drinking a cocktail when they arrived."

"Well, yes. But that's just –"

"So you admit it. What exactly were you celebrating? Getting away with murder?"

"What?"

"Not everyone would find a blood-soaked bathroom something to laugh about," Detective Stanley hissed.

I suddenly felt dizzy. "Blood-soaked?"

"Are you telling me you know nothing about it?"

"Yes! That's *exactly* what I'm saying. I...*I don't believe you!*"

I tried to get up. Detective Stanley took a huge step toward me, making me flinch.

"Where do you think you're going?" he barked.

"To see for myself!"

"Happy to oblige," Detective Stanley snarled. He unlocked the wheelchair with a hard kick, then opened the cottage door and wheeled me to the bathroom door. "Believe me now?" he asked malevolently.

I gasped in horror and disbelief. The bathroom walls were spattered from ceiling to floor in a dark, reddish-brown liquid. The sink was half full of what could only have been blood.

"Cold Cuts!" I cried out.

"So you used a knife," Detective Stanley spat from behind me.

"What?" I screeched. "No!"

"Tell me, Ms. Fremden," he demanded as he whirled the wheelchair around until I was face-to-face with him. "Where's your friend? What have you done with her body?"

"I didn't! I don't! I.... I told you already. I don't know where she is!"

"Uh huh. When was the last time you saw her?"

"This morning. She was in bed. I let her sleep in and I went to the beach, like I said. I came back here to get her for breakfast, but she was still asleep. So I went alone."

"You went to breakfast here at the resort. What time?"

"Around nine."

"Ms. Fremden, I was in the breakfast room at nine. I didn't see you there."

"That's because I didn't go."

Detective Stanley's jaws worked as if he were chewing ground glass. "Which one is it? Did you have breakfast at nine or didn't you?"

"I went in...I saw the back of your toup – *head* – and left. I swear!"

The detective's jowly face took on the color of a ripe pomegranate. "And why would you do *that*, Ms. Fremden?" His sour breath smelled of coffee and cat food, making me glad I hadn't eaten that gross breakfast buffet.

"I...I.... Look, it doesn't matter why I didn't eat breakfast! We need to find my friend. She could be hurt!"

"You think?" Detective Stanley sneered. "Well, now we're getting somewhere. What's your friend's name?"

I started to say Cold Cuts again, but stopped myself in time. I wracked my brain for her real name. *What is it? What is it?*

"Is that a hard question?" the detective sneered.

Crap! I'd only heard Cold Cuts' real name once. And she'd made me promise never to speak it aloud again. *What was it?* Then it popped up in my mind like a toaster pastry. "Penelope." I said. "Penelope Piddle."

Detective Stanley stared at me, incredulous. "Penelope Piddle?"

"Yes."

"Uh huh. So tell me, are you sure it was 'Ms. Piddle' you saw in the bed this morning?"

I thought about it. I'd never actually seen her. "Well, no. But I mean, who else could it have been?"

"Yes. Who else indeed," Detective Stanley said in a tone that made me feel he'd already reached his verdict about me. "When was the last time you saw Ms. Piddle for certain?"

"Last night. We went for a sunset sail. A thunderstorm came up and we got...uh...delayed. We got back really late last night. I left her on the beach with the boat captain."

"Why would you do that?"

"I...uh...they were...*friends*."

"And who is this captain?"

"He works here. He's also the yoga guy."

"Do you know his name?"

"Bilbo Bob, or something like that."

"Bill Robo?"

"Yes, that's it."

"How convenient," the detective sneered.

"What do you mean?"

"It appears that *he's* missing, too."

"What?"

"Where's your vehicle, Ms. Fremden?"

"In the parking lot. It's an RV. But it's not mine. It's Cold...uh...it belongs to Ms. Piddle."

"There's no RV in the parking lot, Ms. Fremden."

"But –"

"Did anyone see you last night who could corroborate your *alleged* sailboat story?"

"No."

"How convenient, *again*."

I slumped in my wheelchair. This was all going to hell in a jet-powered handbasket. "Wait!" I nearly yelled. "There *was* a guy last night who saw me."

"Who?"

"I don't know his name. But I've seen him here twice."

"Can you describe him?"

"Uh...," I cringed. It sounded so weird even I could barely believe it. "He was an old white guy. I couldn't see his face because he was wearing...a beekeeper's hat."

Detective Stanley sucked in a big breath, pursed his lips, then blew it out. "Uh huh. So tell me, if you couldn't see his face, how did you know it was a man?"

"Because of his voice."

"You spoke with him? What did you two talk about?"

"Nothing. He just said something to me."

"And that would be?"

I cringed. "Hard-bodied grubs."

I could almost hear the detective's teeth grind together as he scribbled on his pad. "And tell me, how did you know he was *old?*"

I closed my eyes and forced the words from my lips. "Because besides the beekeeper's hat, he was naked."

Detective slapped his notebook together. "This is absurd! The EMTs said you were laughing and joking like there was a party going on. I didn't want to believe it. You might think this is funny, but believe me, this is no joking matter, Ms. Fremden."

"I don't...I'm not!"

A uniformed cop came running up to the cottage. "Sorry I'm late, sir!" he said.

"I've heard all the drivel I can take from this woman," Detective Stanley told the officer. "Take her down to the station. And call for a CSI unit."

"What?" I cried. "Wait! You've got this all wrong. I need to call my boyfriend. Where's my purse? It must be in my room. Please! Let me get it."

"I'm afraid that won't be possible," Detective Stanley spat. "This room and everything in it is now under investigation as the scene of a homicide. You can call your 'boyfriend' from the police station."

Chapter Fifteen

C rippled, cuffed and about to be incarcerated! The only way this could get any worse was for Tom to see me being hauled away in the back of a police car. So, of course, that's exactly what happened.

"Val!" Tom yelled from across the parking lot. He was dressed for vacation and toting a suitcase. From fifty feet away, I saw his eyes grow as big as poached eggs. "What's going on?" he yelled.

"Tom!" I screeched, as two officers lifted me by the arms from the wheelchair. I took a step toward Tom, forgetting about my ankle. I stepped down and cried out in pain.

"Are you all right?" Tom yelled. He dropped the suitcase and ran toward us.

"Back it up, sir!" one of the cops warned.

Tom stopped dead in his tracks and raised his open palms. "What's going on?" he asked again.

"They think I murdered Penelope!" I screamed as they shoved me into the back seat of a squad car and slammed the door. Tom stood there, mouth open, as the police officers peeled out of the parking lot. When I looked out the rear window, Tom was racing back to his SUV.

I WAS BEGINNING TO feel trapped in the worst customer service call of all time. I'd just been transferred to another department. A new cop had come into the interrogation room, and I'd had to explain my whole story all over again, for the third time. If I hadn't been so worried about Cold Cuts, I would have screamed in frustration.

"I've already told you all I know," I said. The cuffs were off, but my ankle ached and the aspirin the EMT had given me had worn off ages ago. I searched for a glint of mercy in the eyes of jowly faced Detective Stanley, but there was none to be found.

"Well, Lieutenant Borge didn't hear it," Detective Stanley sneered. "So would you be so kind as to start at the beginning?" His eyes made it clear it wasn't a request.

"Like I said before, I don't know where Penelope is," I answered.

"Were you really kicked in the head by a manikin leg?" Borge asked.

"Yes."

"Was that before or after the 'alleged' sailboat ride?"

So much for the good cop/bad cop routine. "Detective Stanley, you were there last night," I argued. "You *saw* us leave to go sailing."

"I saw you both run off toward the beach," he said curtly. "Nothing more."

"But you *know* we went sailing. You can check with Monty at the front desk. I made the reservation with him."

"I spoke with him already," Detective Stanley said. "The clerk said he only saw *you* return last night. He also said you came in with your clothes wet and your hair disheveled. According to him, you were covered in red marks, as if you'd been in some kind of altercation."

Crap! "Look, I know this looks bad, but I can explain...." A commotion outside the interrogation room door caused me to pause mid-sentence. It was Tom's voice, yelling through the wall.

"Tell them you want your attorney!" he bellowed.

"I...I want to speak to my attorney," I said.

"Well, that's it for us," said Borge, blowing out a breath.

Detective Stanley's face went slack and grey as mud. "Take her to a holding cell."

I'D BARELY WARMED THE lumpy cot in my cell when Tom appeared on the other side of the bars. The sight of his face sent a wave of relief washing through me, as if a rope had been thrown to me at the bottom of a well. We talked through the bars while a uniformed cop watched our every move.

"Val," Tom whispered. "Are you okay?"

"Tom! I...I guess so. How did you get in here?"

"I'm a cop, remember?" he said. "And I reminded that Detective Stanley guy that he didn't give you a proper phone call." Tom shot the other cop a look that could melt glass. "Who's this Penelope person they think you murdered?"

"It's Cold Cuts, Tom!"

"What? What happened?"

"Oh, geeze! I went for a walk on the beach this morning...there was this tornado...I got knocked out. When I woke up, there was blood all over the bathroom. Tom, it was horrible! And now Cold Cuts is missing. The cops think I murdered her – that I – *sob* – *ditched her body somewhere!*"

"Geeze, Val! What a mess!"

"I'm sorry, Tom!" I wailed between sobs. "I promise, I didn't do it!"

"What? Good grief, Val! I *know* that. Hold tight. I'm going to make some calls. I should have you out of here in no time."

"But what about Cold Cuts, Tom?"

"Have you tried to call her?"

"No. I couldn't. They wouldn't let me have my purse. It was in the room. I couldn't get back in there."

"Who else has her number?"

"I don't know," I said between sniffles. "I don't think anybody we know does."

"Well, there *is* one thing I already know for sure, Val."

"What, Tom?"

"You can't help her from in there."

TOM WAS TRUE TO HIS word. An hour later, I was released from jail.

"I'm not at all pleased with this," Detective Stanley growled as Tom wheeled me down the hall of the police station. "If anything happens, it's on your head, Lieutenant Foreman."

"I'll take the risk," Tom said. "Your claim against her is all circumstantial. You can't hold her. You *know* that."

"Maybe. But it keeps getting less so by the minute."

I felt a hiccough in the wheelchair's motion. Tom's stride had faltered for a second. "What do you mean?" Tom asked.

"The CSI guy working the scene just called," Detective Stanley said. "He says there's a blood trail leading from the cottage to the beach. And they found a pair of bloody pliers hidden under the mattress – along with what appears to be a human tooth."

"That still doesn't prove anything," Tom said as we reached the exit door.

"Not yet," Detective Stanley said. "But I'm putting a rush on the forensic tests. As soon as they're in, I'm personally going to arrest your 'friend' Ms. Fremden and lock her away for good."

"We'll see about that," Tom hissed, and pushed my wheelchair out the door of the police station. I burst into tears.

"Don't worry about that old blowhard," Tom said as he wheeled me to his SUV. He put on a cheerful face and hoisted me up out of the chair and into the passenger seat. But from the vanity mirror, I saw his face turn grim as he folded the wheelchair and put it in the backseat. He climbed into the driver's seat and shut the door.

"Tom –"

"It's going to be all right," he said, cutting me off. He turned to me, the grimness on his face replaced by determination. "Here. Give me your hand."

"Why?"

Tom sighed. "Just do it, Val. Okay?"

I reached out my hand. Tom took it gently and slipped the sapphire engagement ring back on my finger. "That's better," he said, and kissed me lightly on the lips.

Fresh tears welled in my eyes. "Are you sure you want to get involved with a potential murderer, Tom? What about your career!"

Tom turned the ignition and bit his lip. "We're in this together, Val. Thick or thin."

"I...I don't know what to say, Tom. Thank you?"

"You'd do the same for me." Tom shifted into gear and backed out of the lot.

"So what do we do now?" I asked.

"We're going to see your attorney friend, Mr. Fellows."

"You called him already?"

"Yes," Tom said and shifted into drive. "And I tried to get in touch with Cold Cuts, but then I realized I didn't know her full name. What is it?"

"Penelope Piddle."

Tom stepped on the brake and blew out a breath. "You're kidding, Val. That's what you told them?"

"Yes. Of course. It's the truth!"

"I...I believe you. It's just that...well, it doesn't sound like, you know, a *real* name."

I slumped in my seat. "I know. That's why Cold Cuts asked me never to call her that. The only reason I know it is because she had to sign that contract that time – you know, for that Date Busters deal."

Tom drove out of the lot and headed north. "It just seems so *improbable*," he said, shaking his head. "But that still doesn't explain why this Detective Stanley guy seems so...I dunno...*out to get you*. It doesn't make sense."

"You said it yourself. The story...it's so crazy. You might believe me, but he doesn't."

Tom nodded. "I get that. But why would he want to see to it that you got put away forever?"

I cringed. "Maybe it's because I've seen him with his wig off."

Tom turned and stared at me with a face like melted wax. "Oh Val. Don't tell me."

I bit my lip and cringed some more. "It was an accident."

Tom shook his head and closed his eyes. "What a mess. What a mess."

Chapter Sixteen

"Aren't we going to Mr. Fellows' office?" I asked as Tom pulled his silver 4Runner onto Gulf Boulevard. We'd sat in near silence on the hour-long drive from the Sarasota police station back to St. Petersburg.

"No. He said he'd meet us at your house."

"Oh. That's strange."

Tom shook his head softly and kept his eyes on the road. "After all that's happened today, you think *that's* strange?"

I looked down at my hands.

"It's *Sunday*, Val. He wasn't in his office."

"Oh," I said, and pursed my lips.

Tom turned into Bahia Shores, and then onto Bimini Circle. A shiny white Mercedes was parked in my driveway. Up against poor Shabby Maggie, my old '63 Ford Falcon convertible, the flashy Mercedes stood out like a diamond tiara on a warthog.

Tom pulled up behind the Mercedes. The door flung open and Mr. Fellows climbed out. I'd forgotten how truly short he was. His diminutive frame barely came up to the hood of his fancy car. Dressed in khaki shorts, a pink polo shirt, argyle knee socks and white leather sports shoes, it wasn't the first time he'd reminded me of a lawn jockey.

Tom got out of his SUV, and shook Mr. Fellows' hand. The two exchanged solemn faces. As Tom opened the backseat to get my wheelchair, Mr. Fellows disappeared behind the SUV for a moment. Suddenly, my door flew open. Mr. Fellows was standing there, looking up at me.

"Pardon me if I'm not in full legal regalia," he said, and smiled in a sweet, fatherly way.

"Oh, Mr Fellows, I'm so sorry to bother you with this – especially on a Sunday."

"It's quite all right, Val. As it turns out, I was in the neighborhood."

"Playing golf?" I asked.

Mr. Fellows cocked his silver-haired head. "No. Why?"

"Oh," I said, and wanted to kick myself. "No reason."

"Here we go," Tom said, and wheeled the chair around to my door.

"Oh! Are you injured?" Mr. Fellows asked with genuine concern. "No one told me."

"Just a sprained ankle," I said as Tom lifted me into the wheelchair.

"Well, that's a relief," Mr. Fellows said.

"It sure is," Tom agreed. "Should we get to it? We don't have a lot of time to waste."

We went into the house and Tom propped me up on the couch. Oddly, Mr. Fellows took his shoes off. He grabbed a notepad from his briefcase and tossed it onto the easy chair across from the sofa. Then he climbed up and made himself comfortable in the big, puffy chair. At three feet and change, his stocking feet barely cleared the seat cushion.

"Here you go," Tom said, and put a plate of cookies on the coffee table between us. He handed each of us a mug of coffee, and me a pain pill as well. "Now, I'm off."

"What?" I asked. "Where are you going?"

"I'm on vacation, so I might as well be a tourist at some fancy beach resort," Tom said, trying to sound breezy. "A very *nosy* tourist. Thanks again for coming, Mr. Fellows." Tom shook his hand, then came over and kissed me on the forehead. "Don't worry, Val," he whispered, then disappeared out the door.

Don't worry? Yeah. Like that *was gonna happen.*

"NOW, LET ME MAKE SURE I've understood this correctly," Mr. Fellows said, and peered at me past his bifocals from his nest amongst the pillows on the easy chair.

"Okay," I replied, and straightened myself up on the couch.

"Your room wasn't ready upon your arrival at the resort, so you were given free drinks and a sunset sail as consolation. You and Ms. Piddle went to the bar, drank margaritas and ripped the toupee off Detective James Stanley's head as a joke."

"It wasn't a joke. It was an *accident*. You see, I'd jabbed a toothpick in his hair right before I fell over."

"Right." Mr. Fellows closed his eyes for a second, then scribbled in his pad. "After the toupee incident, a nipple-ringed yoga instructor took you and Ms. Piddle on a cruise. A thunderstorm blew up and you three ended up spending most of the night in a driftwood lean-to on Dog Island."

Mr. Fellows looked up at me. I nodded in agreement. He looked down at his notepad and continued. "Upon your return, you ran into a naked man in a beekeeper's hat. He blinded you with a flashlight and said... ahem...'hard-bodied grubs,' then disappeared into the bushes."

"Correct."

"You went to the lobby and received your room keys from a clerk named Monty. You showered, got in bed, and woke the next day at 5 a.m. with Ms. Piddle snoring in the bed next to yours."

"Yes."

"How was she able to get into the cottage?"

"I left the door unlocked for her."

"And how do you know it was Ms. Piddle in the bed?"

I shrugged. "Uh...I guess because, I mean, who else could it have been?"

Mr. Fellows scribbled on his pad. "Moving on. At around 5:45 a.m., you got coffee from the breakfast room, went for a walk on the beach and read a book in a lounge chair. At 8:45 you returned to the room to find Ms. Piddle still in bed. You went to the breakfast room, saw Detective Stanley there, freaked out and left."

"I never said I freaked out."

Mr. Fellows looked up and winked. "Just seeing if you're paying attention. It sounds like that was a good move on your part."

"If it was, it was the *only* one."

Mr. Fellows peered at me through his glasses for a second. I pursed my lips and sighed. "Then you returned to the beach," he continued. "There, the porter, Brad, told you about another restaurant where you could have breakfast."

"Doug's Dugout."

"Yes. I have it here. You headed in that direction when you were, to use your phrase, 'body-slammed' by a man in the surf, who knocked you down and made you aware of the tornado."

"It was a water spout at the time, but then it turned into a tornado."

"I see. Then you ran back to the resort, stepped in a hole, twisted your ankle and hobbled to cottage number 22. You searched the bed for Ms. Piddle. She wasn't in it. Did you check the bathroom?"

"No."

"Why not?"

"The room started spinning...there wasn't time. I needed to shut the door."

"The bathroom door?"

"No. The door to the outside. The wind was howling and blowing everything around. I tried to close the door, but I couldn't because I could only stand on one foot...."

"And that's when you saw the manikin leg come flying at you. It knocked you out and you woke up with a seagull waddling toward you, ready to peck your eyes out."

"Well, I can't be sure if that was its intentions, but that's what it seemed like to me."

"Okay. Then you called Monty. He called the EMTs. They discovered the blood in the bathroom and called the police. Jim with the bad toupee was the nearest detective available. He arrived, showed you the scene of the crime, then accused you of killing Ms. Piddle."

I hung my head. "Yes. He and another cop took me to the station and questioned me – without giving me a chance to call anyone. Thank goodness Tom saw them putting me in the squad car or I don't know what would have happened."

"How was Tom able to get you out?"

"He told me he showed the cops his badge when he got to the station. That's how he was able to get in the hallway next to the interrogation room. He yelled through the wall for me to ask for an attorney. When I did, they put me in a holding cell until Tom was able to get me out. He told Detective Stanley they didn't have enough to hold me. The guy blew a gasket. But I guess Tom was right, because...well, here I am."

"Like I've told you before, Val. You *do* lead the most interesting life."

"That's one way to put it. So what do you think?"

Mr. Fellows tapped his pen on his notepad. "I think a man's vanity can be a very powerful motivator."

"Not about Detective Stanley. I mean about my story, Mr. Fellows. You do believe me?"

Mr. Fellows head tilted sideways. "Well of course, Val! I have no doubt."

"Thanks."

"And I'm glad you came to me first. Because, I have to say, if I hadn't already been involved with you in that whole debacle a while back concerning the finger you found in your sofa, I'd have never believed one person could be the innocent victim of so much insanity."

I grimaced. "So you think I'm crazy?"

Mr. Fellows smiled and shook his head. "No, Val. I think your *life* is crazy. And what's transpired this time is much more serious than I'm qualified to deal with. As you know, I'm an estate attorney, not a defense attorney. Do you have anyone else you can call to help with your legal representation? Someone familiar with your...uh...*typical life events?*"

I blew out a breath. "I think I *do* know someone. I just wonder if he'll remember *me*."

Chapter Seventeen

As instructed, Mr. Fellows dumped the contents of my nightstand drawer onto the coffee table beside the sofa. Amongst the tissues, nail polish and pens, a few personal items tumbled out onto the wooden table, making me wish I'd thought my plan through a little better beforehand.

"Um...over there," I instructed from my position on the couch. I mentally weighed the pain of my sprained ankle with the excruciating embarrassment I felt at the moment.

"Where?" Mr. Fellows asked as he hovered over the pile of stuff scattered onto the table.

"Next to the pink thing," I pointed. "That yellow scrap from a phonebook."

Mr. Fellows' expression said he'd have preferred to have been wearing rubber gloves. He picked up the scrap of paper from amongst my unmentionables. "This?" he asked.

"Yes. That's it. That's the number for Bernard Charles."

Mr. Fellows studied the paper with a pinched face. "It's an old *Yellow Pages* ad. This says Charles is just a general attorney at law. You're going to need a defense attorney. Someone with enough experience to get you out of this mess."

"That ad is like...I dunno, thirty years old, Mr. Fellows. I found it when I was cleaning the junk out of this place. Mr. Charles has the experience, believe me. And he's no ordinary attorney. He's like some secret government agent or something."

"CIA or FBI?" Mr. Fellows asked, and handed me the torn slip of paper.

"I don't know. And I have a feeling I'm better off not knowing – if you know what I mean."

"I see. Should I leave the room while you make the call?"

"No. Don't be silly." I punched in the number. It didn't ring. Instead, there was a simple recording. "Leave a message," the electronic voice-mail said, then a quick tone sounded. "Um...Mr. Charles. It's Val Fremden. I hate to bother you, but I need your help. Please call me as soon as possible. Uh...thank you. I'm the one with the finger....uh...goodbye."

Mr. Fellows looked at me dubiously. "I guess that's all we can do for now. Should I clean this up?" he waved a hand across the coffee table. I nearly fell off the couch in my haste to answer him.

"Oh! No! Thanks, I'll do it."

"Okay then. I suppose I'll be going. But I'll be in touch."

"Thank you so much."

"You're welcome, young lady," Mr. Fellows said as he was reaching for the doorknob.

The phone rang. "It's Tom," I said. "Hold on. He might have something important to say."

Mr. Fellows turned waited as I punched the speaker button on the phone.

"Hi Tom. Mr. Fellows is here. He was just about to leave."

"Okay. Listen Val. Did you meet anyone at the resort named Freddie?"

"No. I don't think so. Why?"

"I don't know. It may be nothing. But I thought I overheard a maid at the resort saying, "Freddie's done it again.""

"I dunno, Tom. Maybe it's that weird guy in the beekeeper's hat."

"Come on, Val. Think harder. This is getting more serious by the minute."

My stomach flopped. "Why? What's happened?"

"I didn't want to tell you over the phone, but the CSI team found a chunk of...something...washed up on the shore. They said it appears to be human."

"Like a finger?"

"No. Something more...uh...vital."

"Oh, Tom!"

"I know. But it's nothing conclusive. And Val, I just heard from my buddy at the DMV. He ran a search for Penelope Piddle. There's no one in the database that matches that name."

"You can't be serious!"

"Could she have given you a false name?"

"No. I can't believe that. Geeze! Call Milly, Tom. Vance's sister, Annie. She has the records for Date Busters. Maybe I got the name wrong."

"Okay. I'll get on that. Anything new on your end?"

"No, but we've...uh...put some calls out."

"Roger that," Tom said. "I'll see you later this evening."

"Okay. Be careful."

"I will." Tom clicked off the phone.

"This just keeps getting worse and worse," I said to Mr. Fellows.

"Hopefully, that's the end of the surprises," he said. "Sorry to ask, but do you mind if I use your restroom before I go?"

My mind flashed back to the horrific results from the last time I answered that question. I shuddered. "Sure. No problem. You know where it is." I flopped back into the couch, suddenly exhausted. I figured it must be close to midnight, but the clock on the wall said 7:43 p.m. A light tapping on the sliding glass door to my backyard made me look up. Laverne was at the door, waving. I motioned for her to come in.

"I was just watering your plants and saw you on the couch," Laverne said, sticking her head in the door. "What are you doing back here, honey? I thought you were on vacation."

"There's been an accident," I said.

"Oh no! I see your foot's all bandaged up. What happened?" She asked as she walked over for a better look at my foot.

"Hello, Ms. Cowens," Mr. Fellows said.

Laverne jumped like a startled cat. "JD! What are you doing here?"

"Helping out our gal Val. She's in trouble."

"What kind of trouble?" Laverne asked.

"Big trouble," I said. "It's Cold Cuts, Laverne. She went down to the resort with me yesterday. And now...she's disappeared." My voice cracked. Tears filled my eyes. "I've been accused of – *sob!* – murdering her!"

Laverne gasped in horror. Her hand flew to her mouth. "I'm so sorry, Val!" she cried, and ran out the back door.

"Poor Laverne!" I sobbed. "I didn't mean to upset her."

"Don't worry," Mr. Fellows said. "I'll go see about her."

AFTER MR. FELLOWS LEFT, I crawled to the kitchen, grabbed the dusting mop and employed it as a makeshift cane so I could hobble to the bathroom and back. By the time I'd managed it, I was spent. I flopped back on the couch just as the phone rang again. The led screen read, "Unknown Caller." I picked it up.

"Hello?"

"Ms. Fremden?"

"Yes."

"Bernard Charles, at your service."

"You remember me!"

"Of course. How could I forget? Your information about the dirty dog track dealings was invaluable. I owe you one."

"Well, I'm awfully glad you feel that way, because I need a favor. A *big* one. I'm being accused of homicide – of killing a friend of mine. She's missing, and I need you to help me find her." I took a deep breath and prepared to tell all the gory details of my story for the fifth time today, but Mr. Charles spoke before I could say another word.

"No need to explain, Ms. Fremden. I know all about it."

"What? How?"

"Let's just say, we've kind of kept tabs on you since you first blipped onto our radar screen."

"Oh," I said. A sudden chill ran down my spine. *Well, that's not creepy at all....*

"Are you still there?" Mr. Charles asked.

"Yes. I'm sorry. But you haven't...*bugged my house*, have you?"

"Certainly not," Mr. Charles laughed. "But we keep a thumb on the pulse of police activities. Monitor police radios and whatnot."

"Oh." *"Whatnot" indeed.*

"When you called an hour ago, I did a little research before I called back. I don't generally get involved personally with homicide cases unless I'm certain of the innocence of the accused."

"Then you believe me?"

"I read the police report. Even *I* don't have an imagination that good."

"I know it all sounds ridiculous, but I –"

"No need to go on, Ms. Fremden. What I need right now is for you to tell me everything you know about this friend of yours. The one you've been charged with murdering."

"Where should I start?"

"Name. General physical description. Any known aliases or associates."

"Her name is...well, I thought it was Penelope Piddle. But I may have gotten that wrong. Tom's working on it. She goes by the nickname Cold Cuts."

"Well, that's original."

"Yeah. It's a long story."

"And physical attributes?"

"She's female, around thirty years old, and about five-feet five inches tall."

"Race? Hair and eye color?"

"She's brunette. Brown-eyed. Caucasian."

"Known associates?"

"I dunno. But she was getting pretty friendly with a guy at the resort."

"How friendly?"

"As friendly as a person can get."

"I see. And this person's name?"

"Bill Robo. He works at the resort."

"Doing what?"

"Anything that *needs* doing, apparently."

"How about vehicles. Do you know what either one was driving?"

"Yes. Cold Cuts – I mean Penelope drives a 1966 Minnie Winnie RV. White and blue. Florida plates."

"Given the uncertainty over the names, that's pretty specific. It should prove helpful."

"I hope so. But the police say it's gone missing from the resort parking lot. It's the Sunset Sailawa –"

"Yes. I've got that information."

"Wait a minute. You said names, not name."

"Yes. We've done a preliminary search on Bill Robo. It's looking like it might be an alias."

The air went out of me like a punctured tire. "Oh."

"Tell me, Ms. Fremden. Do you know anything about this 'hard-bodied grub' nonsense?"

I felt as useless as humanly possible. "Not a thing."

"Hmm. Perhaps it's some kind of code. Okay then. That's all for now. I've got my team already working on it, Ms. Fremden. In the meantime, the best advice I can give you is to stay out of the fray...and cooperate with the authorities without incriminating yourself."

"If I knew how to do that, Mr. Charles, I wouldn't have bothered you."

Chapter Eighteen

It was dark out when I woke up on the couch. The phone was ringing. I leaned over and grabbed the receiver. My ankle protested in pain.

"Hello?" I said, my voice groggy with sleep.

"Val, it's Milly. Tom called and told me the horrible news. How are you?"

I shifted to sitting up. "As well as can be expected, I guess."

"Listen, I just spoke with Annie. She checked her files. Cold Cuts' name is Piddleton, not Piddle. I wanted you to know right away."

Suddenly, I was wide awake. "Geeze! I'm so glad you did, Milly. Have you told Tom?"

"Not yet. Should I?"

"Yes, if you don't mind. I've got to let a few other people know."

"Okay. Will do. So how are you holding up? Do you need anything?"

"I'm okay. And Tom should be here soon. But thanks for asking. How are things with you and Vance?"

"Fine. Don't worry about us."

"Listen, let's talk tomorrow. I really need to get this news to someone."

"All right. And Val?"

"Yes?"

"I'm really sorry about all this. I hope Cold Cuts is all right."

"Thanks, Milly. Me, too."

I hung up the phone and dialed Bernard Charles. After listening to the mechanical recording, I left a message about Cold Cuts' real name. When I hung up the phone, I felt drained of energy, and nearly empty of hope.

Cold Cuts, where are you?

"VAL."

I opened my swollen, sleepy eyes. The room was pitch black. "Tom?"

"Yes. It's me. I didn't want to scare you. I'm going to turn on a light."

"Okay."

He flipped the switch on the side table lamp, sending white volts shooting through my retinas like lightning bolts.

"I don't know who looks worse. You or me," he joked half-heartedly.

I blinked and squinted as my eyes adjusted to the light. Tom, usually clean, crisp and tidy, looked as if he'd just climbed out of a dumpster after losing a wrestling match with a raccoon.

"Geeze. I hope it's you," I said. "What happened?"

"Nothing worth explaining," he said, then swiped a hand across the coffee table to clear off a space to sit. He sat, grunted, then lifted a butt cheek and pulled something out from under him. "What's this?" he teased, and waggled the pink thing that usually hid out in my night-stand drawer. "You been having fun without me?"

I tried to laugh, but choked instead. "Oh Tom! Please tell me you have good news."

Tom bit his lip. "I wish I did. As you know, Milly called me with Cold Cuts' real name. We ran it through the DMV database and got the plates for the RV. It's not much, but at least it's a start. And no actual body has turned up. So there's hope she's still alive."

"What about that...*piece* of someone they found on the beach?"

"I was hoping you'd forgotten about that."

My body heaved and I burst into loud, ugly crying. Tom leaned in and hugged me. "She's going to be all right," he said, and rubbed my back.

"You don't know that," I sobbed.

"You're right. I don't. But there's nothing more we can do tonight. What you need is a hot shower and a good long sleep."

"I don't want a shower," I protested.

"Trust me on this, Val. You'll feel better. Besides, you really need it." Tom pinched his nose closed with a thumb and forefinger.

A tiny puff of laughter escaped my lips that time, and I let Tom take me up into his arms.

Chapter Nineteen

"Well, I wonder who that could be," Tom said when the doorbell rang. It was barely 6:30 a.m. and Tom was already washing up the cappuccino cups. Neither of us had slept much. We'd both given up and had our coffees before the break of dawn. He'd helped me dress and I was back at my invalid station on the couch, trying not to scratch my mosquito bites.

"What have you done?" I asked.

Tom braced for impact. "I invited Winky and Winnie over to look after you."

"What?" Panic shot through me. I looked down at the coffee table. It was bare. Tom had, thankfully, returned my nightstand drawer and its contents to where they belonged. I folded my arms and scowled. "I don't need looking after. Besides, I've got *you*."

"No you don't. I need to go see what I can find out."

I pouted. "I know. But *Winky?*"

Tom shrugged apologetically. "I tried for Winnie, but they come as a set, apparently."

The doorbell rang again. Tom took a step to answer it.

"Wait!" I cried out.

"What now?" Tom asked.

I lowered my voice as if the pair were already in the room. "What do they know?"

Tom smiled wistfully. "Nothing. Except that you're a little down in the dumps and could use a friend. After all, you twisted your ankle *on vacation*, remember? That's all the story they need to know for now."

"Okay," I sighed. "Let them in."

"Hey there, Val Pal!" Winky hollered as he came through the door. He was carrying a length of polished bamboo and a huge tackle box. Winnie was toting a box of Davie's Donuts. I hoped they weren't recycled.

"What are you two going to do?" I asked. "Beat me with a stick and force-feed me donuts?"

"Well now, that depends on your behavior," Winky joked. "And how quick you learn them new tricks."

"Don't listen to him," Winnie said as Tom and Winky laughed. "He's made you a cane out of an old fishing rod." She twisted her lips and shook her head at Winky, then turned to Tom. "Won't you stay and have a donut with us?"

"I really need to get going," Tom said. "But can I take one for the road?"

"Sure," Winnie beamed and pushed her red-frame glassed up on her pudgy little nose. "I picked them up fresh this morning."

"That was mighty nice of her, wasn't it, Val?" Tom said as he grabbed a crème filled donut and wagged his eyes at me.

I glared back at Tom. "Yes, is sure was." I nodded at Winnie and Winky. "Thank you for the donuts...and for keeping me company."

"You three have fun," Tom said, his hand on the knob of the still-open door. Before he disappeared, he winked at me and smiled, and I forgot for a second about the terrible situation we were in.

MY KITCHEN COUNTER looked like a flea-market stall. Besides a cane and donuts, Winnie and Winky had brought along enough fishing tackle to fill a clothes hamper.

"I hope you don't mind if we work while we're here," Winnie said from her perch on a barstool.

"Not at all. It looks kind of interesting."

"Yeah, it's fun," said Winnie. "And the money's good, too."

"Sure beats that time I was a male stripper," Winky said. He held up a rubber worm and waggled it lasciviously. "Still, it was good money. I earned thirty bucks in one shot."

"You were a stripper?" I grimaced. "I don't mean to be rude, but...who would pay to see *you* naked?"

"Look who's talkin', you old, one-legged, flea-bitten varmint."

"Winky!" Winnie scolded.

Winky sat up straight on his barstool and poked his freckled nose in the air. "For your information, Miss Know-It All, I wasn't *naked*. I wore me a Speedo. And the old gals at the nursing home seemed to appreciate it. Paid me a dollar each at the door."

"To get out, I bet." I shook my head in disgust at the thought. "I'm surprised you weren't arrested."

Winky laughed. "Who says I wasn't? Jail ain't too bad for a day or two. Three squares and a workin' john."

"Enough, already," I begged. "Why are you telling me this?"

"'Cause you asked." Winky turned to Winnie for support. "*She* started it."

"Well, I'm *stopping* it, too," I said. "Show me your stuff."

Winky got up and started to waggle his hips and pull off his shirt.

"I meant your *tackle* stuff!"

Winky grinned. "I know. I was just funnin' ya. Don't get your panties all in a wad."

"I won't," I said, and sat up. I grabbed the homemade bamboo cane and tapped it on the floor. It seemed sturdy, so I hoisted myself up on it."

"Lazarus back from the dead," Winky joked.

"Ha ha," I sneered, and hobbled over to the kitchen counter to see what they were working on. "Wow. Who knew there were so many lures?"

"I did," Winky said.

"This one's my favorite," Winnie said. She held up a lure that looked like a tiny, white feather duster with a red dot at the top and a crimson band around its neck. "It's called a pop-eye buck-tail jig."

I shook my head. "That's the dumbest thing I ever heard."

"No worse than y'all's names for nail polish," Winky shot back. "What was that one you liked, Winnie? Princess Delilah's Dreams or some such nonsense."

"Princess Pink," Winnie said. She put down an earring she'd just finished. "Well, that's it for me. I've got to go. My shift at Davie's starts in fifteen minutes." She looked over at Winky. "You two behave, now. No monkey business. You hear me?"

Winky flashed his girlfriend a mischievous smile as she picked up her purse and brushed donut crumbs off her lap.

"What?" I asked. "You're leaving us?"

"I'm afraid so, Val. Consider yourself lucky. At least he's potty-trained now."

"Hardy-har-har," Winky sneered playfully. "It'll be fun, Val. You can help me make earrings." He held a pair of lime-green jelly worms to his ears and rolled his eyes around like a lunatic.

"Great. I'm stuck in a vocational re-training scheme with *One Flew Over the Cuckoo's Nest*."

"You'll survive," Winnie laughed, and closed the door behind her.

I sat down in the stool Winnie had been occupying. "What's that chubby white one called? The one with the red eye?"

"Hate to break it to you," Winky answered, "but you're lookin' in the mirror."

It was hard, but I forced myself not to laugh. "Come on!"

"It's called a spook. It's good for catching lunkers.

"What's a lunker?"

"It's a freshwater bass."

"Why don't they just call it that then?"

"Well, it's a special kind a bass," Winky explained. "That's the name they give 'em when they done got old and wily and hard to hook." Winky studied me for a moment and laughed. "Kinda like you, Val. And they got a big old mouth on 'em like you, too."

"Thanks," I said, surprised at how his words stung. I got up and took a step toward the couch.

"Now don't be sore, Val. I was just funnin'."

"And *you're* so easy to hook?" I pouted and flopped back on the couch. "Have you asked Winnie to marry you?"

"Not exactly. But I'm studyin' on the idea." Winky got up and stood on the other side of the coffee table. "Can I see yore ring?"

I held out my hand.

"No, I mean see it. Hand it over."

"Ugh. Why?" I tugged the ring from my finger.

"Winnie said she really liked it. Wants me to dublicate it."

"Duplicate," I said, handing him the ring.

He studied it under the ceiling light. "I mean make a double of it Val. That's called dublication."

"Fine. Should be easy now that you're a jewelry maker." I scratched absently at a bite on my arm.

"I ain't that good yet," Winky said, and handed me back the ring. "Tom told me you done gone and twisted yore ankle. But how'd you get all them bug bites? I believe I seen guys livin' in cardboard boxes looked better'n you."

"You're just full of compliments today," I sneered.

"I do what I can." Winky fell back into the easy chair. "So what *really* happened on vacation? You and Tom get in a brawl?"

"No," I said, suddenly on the verge of tears again. "Just my regular crap luck is what happened."

Winky's wisp of a ginger eyebrow perked up. "What do you mean? I thought you said you and Tom wasn't –"

The phone rang. I lurched at the receiver.

"Hello?"

"Well, there you are," said a voice from my past. One I'd hoped I'd never hear again. It was the slimy voice of the ambulance-chasing, Hummer-driving jerk-wad attorney who'd tried to extort money from me over the finger I'd found in my couch a couple of years ago.

"I've been trying to reach you on your cell phone, but you didn't answer," Ferrol Finkerman sneered. "I'm surprised you still have a land line. To be honest, I'm even more surprised that you *answered* it. It's like a flashback to the good old days when, if someone picked up the phone, you knew exactly where they were."

I put my hand over the receiver. "This is private, Winky."

Winky shrugged. "Okay. I'll just take a turn at your crapper, then."

"Sure. Go ahead." He hauled himself up and disappeared down the hall.

"What do you want, Finkerman?"

"Well, money, of course."

"Have you lost your mind?"

"No, but apparently *you* have. Attacking a poor man in public and causing deep psychological trauma. Mmmm. I can smell the dollar bills."

"What are you talking about?"

"You've gone and ticked off the wrong man, Ms. Fremden."

"And who would that be?"

"Besides me, you mean? Why, Detective James Stanley. A close, personal friend."

I groaned. This was the last thing I needed right now. But somehow, my new-found anger and disgust melded together and formed a glue strong enough to hold me together. "Why am I not surprised?"

"Well, that makes one of us. I have to say, I didn't think you had it in you."

"To trip and fall and accidently knock someone over?"

"No. Not that. I mean to stab someone to death. Stanley showed me the pics. Nobody could have survived that scene. It looked like the Bates Motel."

"Shut up!"

"And your luck just keeps getting better, Ms. Fremden. Because I'm going to make sure you're served with my client's claim before you end up in the slammer."

"You're a jackass, you know that, don't you?"

"And I'm just down the street," Finkerman said. "See you in a minute."

Chapter Twenty

rap! I was being held prisoner in my own home by a freckle-faced, fishing-tackle jeweler who didn't have the faintest inkling about what kind of trouble I was in. And now that skinny-assed, frizz-head Ferrol Finkerman was barreling toward my house in his stupid, canary-yellow Hummer. There was no time for explanations. I only hoped there was time to escape.

"What's with the blue toilet bowl?" Winky asked as he emerged from the hallway.

"Ty D Bol," I said, and hauled myself off the couch to standing with the help of Winky's homemade cane. "It's my turn for the bathroom," I said, and lumbered up to him. "This might take a while."

Winky snorted. "And you're always sayin' *I* ain't got no couth."

I needed to keep Winky distracted somehow. "There's beer in the fridge," I said, and pushed by him. "Help yourself."

"Thanks. Don't mind if I do."

I hobbled down the hall, past the bathroom to my bedroom. I shut the door behind me and fished around inside my nightstand drawer until I found the spare key to Shabby Maggie. That was the easy part. Now I had to sneak out the window. Thankfully, the windowsill was low – about level with the middle of my thigh. I hoisted the window pane up and pushed out the screen. Then I stuck a hand on the wall, balanced on my good right foot and stuck my left leg out the window.

I straddled the windowsill and stuck the cane in the grass. Then I tried to haul the other half of me out the window without putting pressure on my left foot. Yeah. Like that was going to work. I lost my balance and fell onto the lawn. The impact knocked the key out of my hand.

You've got to be kidding me! Finkerman could be here any second!

I scrambled around on my knees, clawing at the grass like a cat with diarrhea and no litter box in sight. Finally, my fingers found pay dirt. I plucked the key from the lawn, propped myself up on the cane and hauled myself to standing. Then I hobbled as fast as I could to the car, opened the door, backed my butt up to the seat and fell inside. Beads of sweat poured down my face as I hit Maggie's ignition switch. Her twin glass-pack mufflers roared to life.

The front door flew open and Winky hollered at me. "Hey! Where you going?"

"To get lunch," I said, and shifted into reverse. "I'll be back in a little bit!" I hit the gas and peeled down the driveway. I didn't have a phone, license *or* wallet, but, thanks to Winky, I had a bamboo cane I could use to beat Finkerman about his ugly, frizzy-haired head.

Halfway down the block I passed the obnoxious lawyer in his hideous yellow Hummer. He stared at me as if he'd seen a ghost, then slammed on the brakes. Thank goodness those overblown dune buggies had a turning radius of a quarter mile. I punched the gas on Maggie's V8 and disappeared in the cloud of blue smoke pouring from her chattering muffler.

I didn't know what was wrong with Maggie, but she'd begun burning oil like a bad fry cook. She coughed and sputtered, and I pulled into the next street and ducked down an alleyway. With no money, nowhere to go, and no other ideas, I sat in the alley and waited. About twenty minutes later, I was chased out by an old man in a Lincoln Town Car. I was blocking his access.

I turned the ignition on Maggie and limped home like a busted teenage runaway.

"I DIDN'T KNOW YOU WAS related to Harry Houdini," Winky snarled as I hobbled back through my front door. He set an empty beer bottle on the counter. "I'm supposed to be keepin' an eye on you, you know."

"I know."

"So, where's lunch?"

"I forgot I didn't have any money."

"Uh huh. Somethin' fishy's goin' on around here. And I got the evidence."

I sighed. What was the harm in telling him now? I opened my mouth to confess the whole horrible mess, but Winky cut me off.

"What was this doing on your couch?" He held up a round, opaque disk the size of a jar lid.

"What is that?"

"This here's a tarpon scale, I do believe. What I wanna know is, how'd it get on your couch?"

"How should I know? I don't even know what a tarpon *is*."

"It's a fish, you lunker."

"Not this again, Winky. I'm not in the mood." I plopped back onto the couch.

"What's the matter with you, Val? You're always good for a round of word wrasslin'. Something really *is* wrong, ain't it?"

I pursed my lips and shook my head.

"Don't be a soiled brat, Val."

"Spoiled."

"What's spoiled?" he asked, and sat on the coffee table beside me. "Don't you trust me?"

"It's not that, Winky," I confessed. "It's just...I don't know what to say. I don't know where to begin."

Winky patted me on the hand. "Well, like ol' Laverne always says, begin at the beginin.'"

I GAVE WINKY THE ABBREVIATED version. I started with the tornado and ended with Cold Cuts missing. I didn't mention Bill Robo or the bloody bathroom.

"Is that all?" Winky laughed. "I bet she just run off with one of them young fellers she met at the beach."

"I hope you're right."

"Cold Cuts ain't as cautious as you, Val. It's took you what? A good *two years* to warm up to me and the other fellers."

He had a point. "That's true. But unlike her, I've had my heart crushed more than once or twice. She's too young to know any better." Melancholy threatened to set me off on another crying jag. I needed something to occupy my mind besides thoughts of Cold Cuts being tied up somewhere...or worse. "Show me how to make a pair of earrings," I said to Winky.

He grinned like a carnival barker. "Make me a baloney sandwich and I'll show you how to make our best seller. Seems like I got to go twiced a week now to Old Joe's Bait Shack to refill the little display thingy. "

"Really?" I looked across the kitchen counter at the tackle box and jumbles of lures, wires and jewelry fasteners. "Which one is that?"

"Like the ones me and Winnie give you for your birthday," Winky said. He picked up a handful of small, colorful lures that looked like a stubby, pregnant worms. "The ones that use these here hard-bodied grubs."

"What did you say?"

"The ones that –"

"I *heard* you!" I said, and hobbled to the phone.

"Then what in tarnation did you ask –"

"Shhh!" I picked up the receiver to call Tom, but a flash of movement in the driveway made my heart leap with fear. *Finkerman!* I peeked out the window, but it wasn't a yellow Hummer I saw. It was a silver 4Runner. Tom was home.

"Tom!" I cried out when he walked in the door. "Winky has some news for you!"

"Huh?" Tom said, taken aback by my verbal assault.

"Tell him, Winky. About the earrings!"

"Well, he already knows," Winky said. "We're makin' earrings outta fishing tackle and sellin' 'em at –"

"Arrgghh!" I groaned in frustration. "Tom. My earrings. They're made from hard-bodied grubs."

"I'm sorry, Val," Tom said. "What are you talking about?"

Winky shot me a smug sneer.

"The old guy in the beekeeper's hat, Tom. Hard-bodied grubs. That's what he kept saying to me. He must be some kind of fisherman."

"Well, he *was* wearing fishing gear, Val," Tom said. "So I guess that makes sense."

My excitement evaporated. "Oh. I guess you're right. I thought it might have been a clue. Crap. I guess it wasn't."

"I know you're trying to help, Val," Tom said, taking my hand. "But the best thing you can do right now is stay off that foot and out from under the hair of – ugh – *away* from Detective Stanley. Can you do that for me?"

A few hours ago, I could have easily complied. But now that Finkerman was in the picture, it was practically an impossibility. "I'll try," I offered.

"Try hard," Tom said to me sternly, then softened his tone. "Remember, Cold Cuts has only been missing for a day."

My mouth fell open. "Only a *day?* Geeze! It feels like a year!"

"No. Only about thirty hours, Val. Anything's still possible. The preliminary results of the CSI tests should start coming in tomorrow. Hopefully they'll start to clear some of this up."

"CSI?" Winky asked. "Nobody told me nothin' about no crime stuff investigators!"

Tom shot me an apologetic grimace. "Winky," Tom said. "Why don't you and I go out for a beer? I'll tell you more about what's going on, then drop you at Davie's Donuts after."

"All right. That sounds good to me."

Tom squeezed my hand. "Can I get you anything while I'm out?"

"Just another box of tissues and a bottle of Tanqueray."

Tom kissed me on the forehead. "I'll be back in an hour with something for dinner."

"Thanks," I said.

As he headed out the door with Winky, my land line began to ring. "Go on, I'll get it," I said. Tom nodded and closed the door behind him. I read the name on the phone's LED display and yanked the cable from the wall.

Chapter Twenty-One

The spicy green curry Tom brought home for dinner last night woke me up at 1:03 a.m. Tom lay sound asleep beside me, seemingly impervious to the wrath of the chili pepper gods. I stared at the clock on my nightstand and listened to his rhythmic breathing.

I wondered if Cold Cuts was still breathing, too.

Tears welled in my eyes. To keep from blubbering, I made myself concentrate on recalling, in detail, the conversation Tom and I had shared over supper last night.

"Winky told me about you sneaking out to get lunch," Tom had said. I remembered how his eyes had been mixed with suspicion and curiosity. "I thought to myself, now why would you do that? Val, is something going on?"

I'd lied to him. "Tom, I was stuck with Winky all day. I needed a break."

Tom had believed me, or at least pretended he did, and changed the subject. "I wanted to talk to you about the guy in the beekeeper's hat. I asked around today and the resort. No one else has seen him."

I'd gotten defensive. "I *know* I saw him, Tom. I didn't make it up. Cold Cuts saw him, too."

"I'm not saying you made it up, Val."

"Then what *are* you saying?"

"Listen, this isn't a 'me-against-you' situation here. I'm on *your* side."

I'd immediately felt like a turd. "I'm sorry. It's just...I'm so worried about Cold Cuts."

"I know. Me, too. So help me out here. Work *with* me, not against me."

"Okay. I'm sorry. You're right. So, what does it mean, that no one but Cold Cuts and I saw this guy? Is he a ghost or something?"

"No," Tom had said. "You told me he was a big guy, right? Do you think he's strong enough to take on Bill Robo?"

"I don't know. He was old. But he looked pretty big. And he was in good shape. *All over.*"

Tom had let that one slide. "You ran into him along the trail that night after the sailboat ride."

"Well, more like I spotted him in the bushes."

"Right. If you hadn't, I wonder if things would have turned out differently."

"What do you mean, Tom?"

"I just wonder if he might have been planning on watching you pass, then sneaking up behind you and abducting you."

Chills had run through my body. "You think *I* was his intended target?" I'd asked. "You think when I spotted him there in the bushes, he changed his plans and went after Cold Cuts instead?"

"I dunno," Tom had said. "It's just a theory."

"He blinded me with a flashlight, but he didn't try to grab me or anything. Why would he do that, then let me go and take Cold Cuts instead?"

"Maybe he saw the three of you come off the boat together. He waited on the trail until the odds got better. Two against one isn't great, but it's better than three against one."

"Two against one?"

"Cold Cuts and Bill Robo."

"You think he got them *both?*"

"Maybe. Did Cold Cuts have the keys to the RV with her?"

I'd thought about it for a moment. "Yes. I mean, I'm pretty sure. We couldn't get in the room yet. All she'd brought for luggage was some grocery bags. I don't think she'd leave the keys in them. Why do you ask?"

"From what you've told me, that old fisherman is a sketchy character, at best."

"He's probably psycho."

"Right," Tom had said. Then his face had gone deadly serious. "I'm just thinking out loud here, Val. But the guy could have blinded Cold Cuts and Bill with the flashlight, like he did you. Then threatened them with a knife – or a gun – and forced them to drive him somewhere in Glad's old RV."

"That makes sense...but Tom, I sure hope you're wrong."

"Me, too, Val. Me, too."

THE THOUGHT THAT COLD Cuts could have been abducted by the psycho fisherman made me antsy. I was still lying beside Tom, thinking about waking him up when his phone alarm went off. He rolled over and gave me a gentle bear hug. "Did you get any sleep?"

"Not as much as you."

"Well, you can nap today," Tom said and kissed me on the forehead. "I'm going to fix us a couple of cappuccinos, then I'm taking off to Sarasota to see what I can find out."

He started to roll away, but I held him tight. "Let me come with you."

"No can do. You need to rest that ankle."

"I've got a cane. I can manage."

"Yeah. Winky told me how you 'managed' to sneak out the window and drive off. Please don't do that again."

"What's the big deal?"

"You need to *rest*, Val. Not to mention that your car is running like crap, and you don't even have a cell phone when you get into trouble."

"Don't you mean *if* I get in trouble?"

Tom gave me a look that made me sigh in defeat. I let go of him and rolled onto my back. "When will I get my phone back?"

"I don't know. I'm going back down to the station today. I'll check." Tom sat up onto the edge of the bed.

"Let me come along, Tom. I promise I'll be good."

Tom stood up and winked at me. "Sorry. But I don't need your help today. *Or* your promises. I've got *insurance.*"

"What do you mean?"

Tom grinned and waggled his blond eyebrows. "Goober's coming over to make sure you stay out of trouble."

"Tom! How could you?" I bellowed. I grabbed a pillow and threw it at him. He laughed and ducked out the door.

Chapter Twenty-Two

Frustration descended on me like a shroud as I watched my handsome, blond, hard-working cop walk out the door and a bald, peanut-headed deadbeat walk in. Goober must have read between the lines on my face.

"Good morning to you, too, Val," Goober laughed. "It's not a death sentence, you know."

"Speak for yourself," I snarled. "There's coffee in the pot. Help yourself."

Goober bowed and tipped an imaginary hat. "Thanks for your hostility."

I snickered despite myself. "Sorry. I just...I feel so *useless*. I want to help, but –"

"Your phone's unplugged," Goober said, cutting me off. He reached down and plugged it back into the wall.

"If it rings, don't answer it," I said.

Goober looked me up and down.

"I'm going to the ladies' room," I said. I didn't really have to go. At least not that badly. It was a ploy to escape Goober's questioning eyes. He had a way of seeing right through me that was disconcerting, to say the least. Plus, I figured I might as well use the facilities while they were still Ty D Bol fresh.

When I returned to the living room, Goober was at the kitchen counter, slurping coffee and yacking on his cellphone. His words set my heart to thumping.

"Was there any blood?" he asked, and furrowed his bushy eyebrows. "Clothes in a heap outside?"

Goober caught my worried look and rolled his eyes as if to say I shouldn't worry. "Food smell like rat poison?" he asked the person on the other end of the line. "How about your guitar? Was it smashed to smithereens?"

I flopped on the couch and pretended to read a magazine as I eavesdropped.

"Uh huh," Goober said. "Well, as I see it, you might still have a chance." He clicked off the phone and shook his head in disgust. "*Romance*. Who needs it?"

"Who were you talking to?" I asked.

Goober twisted his lips, making his caterpillar mustache undulate. "This guy I know. He and his wife are having a so-called *lover's quarrel*." Goober had sneered and formed air quotes with his fingers when he'd said the last two words.

"What happened?"

"The usual." Goober took another swig of coffee and walked from behind the kitchen counter. "His wife told him to get out last night. He went back this morning, and the old gal wasn't there. He called me wondering if he still had a chance with her. Pathetic, right?"

"And your advice was along the lines of, if she hadn't destroyed all of his stuff and tried to poison him, he was probably good to go?"

Goober sat in the easy chair with a sigh. "Sure. You should know that, Val. You've been married before."

I shook my head and laughed. "Fair enough. So, what's going on with Jorge? Why didn't he come with you?"

"He's at some relaxation thing."

"Huh?"

"Tom didn't tell you?"

"No."

Goober seemed pleased at the fact I didn't know. "It's like a retreat, Val. You know, for people to learn how to calm their own nerves and deal with jerks. It's called *Give Me Serenity* or some such horse hockey as that."

"I take it you don't think it's a good idea," I said.

Goober rolled his eyes.

"How do you think Jorge did on his tests?" I asked.

Goober shrugged his big shoulders. "Who knows? What I want to know is what's up with you and Cold Cuts. Winky said she ran off and left you at the beach."

My gut flipped over. "You *know*?"

The land-line rang. My stomach did a summersault. I glanced at the display and my internal organs completed an Olympic gymnastics routine.

"Aren't you going to get that?" Goober asked.

"No."

Goober eyed the phone, then me. "What's *Finkerman* calling about?"

I flinched. "That depends. What do you already know?"

Goober's bushy eyebrows met in the middle of his forehead. "Is this some kind of game show, Val? *What's My Crime?* I'm not going to sit here and guess. Tell me. What's going on?"

The phone kept ringing. "Goober, it's too horrible to explain."

Goober's face softened. "Val, you're talking to a man who lives on a full-time basis with Winky and Jorge. What could be more horrible than that?"

I bit my lip and sighed. "I guess you've got a point there."

WHILE WE POLISHED OFF the leftover Chinese takeout from last night, I spilled most of the beans to Goober.

"We don't know Bill Robo's real name, or the identity of this fisherman guy. Hell, Goober, we don't even know how long Cold Cut's has been missing."

"Why not?" Goober asked, then stuck a chopstick full of spicy beef and noodles into the gaping hole underneath his moustache.

"Because I don't know for sure if it was even Cold Cuts in the bed next to mine."

"Well, I can tell you, it wasn't."

"What do you mean?"

"Cold Cuts doesn't snore."

I dropped a chopstick. "How do you know *that?*"

Goober snorted. "And no one thinks I can keep a secret."

Two and two added up in my mind, and I nearly dropped my little cardboard takeout box. "Oh my lord! You and.... *No!* That means...you...spent the night with Cold Cuts, and I spent the night with...who knows who! Maybe *a murderer!*" I wasn't sure which thought horrified me more.

Goober shrugged. "I dunno if you could make *that* big a leap, Val. Maybe you should leave the deducing up to Tom." Goober looked up at the window behind me. "Speak of the devil, here he comes now."

Goober grinned slyly and dumped the rest of the takeout container into his mouth. I turned and looked out the window. Tom's silver 4Runner was pulling into the driveway. I whipped back around to face Goober. He was munching on a mouthful of food like a bald chipmunk.

"Goober! Tom doesn't know about Finkerman yet. I want to keep it that way for now."

Goober smiled, causing the noodle caught in his moustache to fall into his lap. "Don't worry, Val," he mumbled through his mouthful of food. "Your secret's safe with me."

"I'VE GOT GOOD NEWS and not-so-good news," Tom said as he sat down on the couch beside me. Goober and I looked at each other like kids waiting outside the principal's office for a paddling.

"I pulled some strings," Tom said, "and was able to get one of the guys doing the investigation down in Sarasota to tell me what he knows. Anyway, it turns out that the glob of flesh they found on the beach wasn't human after all. It was sea pork."

"Sea pork?" Goober and I asked simultaneously.

"Yeah," Tom said, then tried to explain. "It's kind of complicated, but basically that's what they call these little sack-like things in the coral reefs. They live together in globs. Anyway, when they die, they turn grey and sometimes end up washing up on the beach, looking a lot like a chunk of human brain tissue."

"So the stuff they found," I said. "It wasn't human."

"Right," Tom said. "And there's more good news. The blood all over the bathroom wasn't blood. It was some sort of corrosive chemical compound."

I nearly jumped in Tom's arms. "So that means Cold Cuts wasn't murdered!"

Tom fended off my embrace. "Not so fast, Val. We don't know that for sure. She's still missing. Right now, this only means that she probably wasn't killed in the room."

My hopes sunk as fast as they'd risen. "Oh."

"You said there was bad news," Goober said.

Tom sucked in a breath and let it out. "The blood on the pliers they found under the mattress was human. The tooth, was, too. And the blood trail leading from the cottage to the beach was a mixture of human and fish blood."

"The fisherman!" I cried out.

Tom nodded. "There's been no trace of him, Cold Cuts, or this Bill Robo guy since the incident."

"What does that mean, Tom?" I asked.

"It's really too soon to say," Tom answered. "I just wanted to tell you face-to-face what I found out, before I head back to the resort."

"What are you gonna do down there?" Goober asked.

"I'm gonna see what else I can find out about this Bill Robo character. He worked there, after all. Hopefully, they did a background check on him. But maybe not. I mean, with all the illegal aliens here in Florida. It's not a given. I'm also going to write down all the license plates in the lot. If Robo took off with Cold Cuts in her RV, his vehicle ought to still be in the lot."

"Unless he used alternate transportation," Goober said. "He could have taken the bus or a bicycle. Or hitched a ride with a friend."

"Goober's right," I said. "As weird as Robo was, I wouldn't be surprised if he rode there on a magic carpet."

My land-line rang again. Goober locked eyes with me.

"Aren't you going to get that?" Tom asked.

Goober glanced at the display. "Telemarketer," he lied.

I turned to Tom and smiled, then practically pushed him off the couch. "I think your idea about the plates is brilliant, Tom. The sooner you get going, the sooner you can get back here."

Chapter Twenty-Three

My land line rang off and on all afternoon. I'd wanted to unplug it, but Goober insisted otherwise. He looked up from the paper and checked the phone's display for what seemed like the hundredth time.

"Finkerman again," he said. "Answer it and get it over with, Val. It doesn't pay to postpone the inevitable."

"Ugghh!" I scowled and reached for the receiver. I put it to my ear. "Finkerman?" I got back nothing but dial tone. I smiled smugly. "Oh well. Too bad."

Goober grunted out a laugh.

"Goober, do you think a person's life is fated by their name?"

"What do you mean?"

"I was just thinking about something Finkerman told me once. When I asked him why he does what he does for a living. He told me with a name like Ferrol Finkerman, he was doomed to be a jerk."

"It's a theory. But then, how do you explain all the other ambulance chasers?"

"Huh. Good point." I sunk back into the couch.

"Finkerman sucks as a name, sure," Goober said. "But it's hard to forget – unlike Gerald Jonohhovitz.

"Gerald who?"

"Exactly."

"Goober...is that your real name?"

"Unfortunately, yes."

"So you think it's true? A bad name can scar you for life?"

"I dunno about *scarring*, but do I think it can limit your possibilities? Sure."

"It doesn't seem to have affected Sir Henry P. Rockbottom, III, or whatever his name was."

"Who's that?"

"The guy who built the Sunset Sail-Away Beach Resort."

Goober whistled long and low. "Lucky sap. I'd like to see what he'd have accomplished with a name like Goober. I can't tell you what a positive effect it's had on my life experience thus far."

I laughed. "Then why do you keep it?"

Goober smiled wistfully beneath his fuzzy moustache. "Because Glad gave it to me."

I choked up and nodded. We both sat in silence for a few minutes, until I cleared the cloud of memories with a question.

"A friend once told me that 'The Bills of this world will survive.' What do you think she meant by that?"

"Easy," Goober said, and held up two fingers. "There's only two things you can't escape in this world. Death and *bills*."

I sighed. "I guess that makes about as much sense as anything does. You hungry? Those Chinese leftovers didn't last."

"I could eat again."

"Champ's Pizza?"

"Sure," Goober winked. "I like the name."

GOOBER AND I HAD FALLEN asleep to a riveting program on PBS about mollusks on the move. The sound of Tom coming through the door woke both of us.

"Hey," I said from the couch. "How did it go?"

"Mixed bag," Tom said. "I need a beer. Hey, Goober. You're free to go now."

"Just when it's getting good?" he joked, and rubbed his eyes.

"One beer," he said to Goober. "I'll catch you up with what I know, then I'm heading to bed. I'm beat."

Tom grabbed a couple of beers and joined Goober and me in the living room. He sat beside me on the couch and took a long draw from his beer before he spoke.

"So? What did you find out?" I asked.

"The cottage had a professional cleaning job before you were allowed in it, Val."

"How do you know that?"

"The CSI report. They sprayed the cottage with Luminol."

"Lumi what?"

"Luminol. It's a chemical that makes any traces of blood present glow under a black-light. Anyway, they sprayed the cottage with it, and when they turned off the lights, the room lit up like the Milky Way Galaxy."

"But...whatever happened in there had to have happened *before* Cold Cuts disappeared," I said.

"Right," Tom said. "But on the drive home, it made me think twice about what that maid had said about 'Freddie doing it again.'"

"That's why they kept delaying our check in," I said, and collapsed into the sofa cushions. "Someone had killed someone in there the night before. Geeze, Tom. What's going on at that resort?"

Tom shook his head. "I don't know. It could be a related homicide or a coincidence. Florida doesn't have a reputation for craziness for nothing."

"Well, on that note, I think I'll take my leave," Goober said. "I'll let you two get some shuteye." He stood up, then paused. "I'm really sorry about all of this."

"Thanks, Goober," Tom said. "Drive safely."

As Goober headed out the door, Tom turned to me. "At least there's *one* good development."

I perked up. "What's that?"

Tom reached into his breast pocket. "I got your phone back." He handed me my cellphone. "Apparently, the only people you call are me and Champ's Pizza. At least I know who my competition is, now."

I smiled weakly and grabbed the phone. "Thanks, Tom."

"Now I just have one question for you."

"What?"

"Why do you have thirteen text messages on your phone from Ferrol Finkerman?"

I bit my lip and sighed. "Grab me another beer and I'll tell you everything."

Chapter Twenty-Four

I tried to convince Tom that my ankle was better by getting up and limping to the kitchen to make cappuccinos the next morning. He didn't buy it. When he caught me hobbling around with my cane like an old lady, he scolded me like a naughty puppy.

"Get back in bed, crazy woman," he'd demanded playfully, and kissed me on the cheek.

Any other time, I'd have taken it as foreplay. But my yelping ankle reminded me he wasn't angling for a tryst.

"All right. I give up," I'd said, and set the can of espresso on the counter.

"You have to learn to let other people take care of you sometimes," Tom had said. "Now get off that ankle."

"Yes, sir," I'd said, and hobbled back to bed.

"YOU KNOW I LOVE YOU, don't you?" Tom asked as he slipped on his loafers and prepared to leave for Sarasota.

"Yes," I answered. "Why do you ask?"

"You have to learn to trust me more. To share your problems with me. Like Finkerman. No more secrets, okay?"

"Finkerman wasn't really a secret. I was just waiting for the best time to tell –"

"I mean it, Val. I'm serious."

"Are you saying you don't have any secrets from me?" I asked, and brushed Tom's bangs from his forehead.

"No."

"What about Jorge? You took him to a retreat. You didn't tell me."

Tom scrunched his nose. "Oh. I thought I did. With everything else going on, I guess I forgot. How'd you find out?"

"Winky."

Tom's lips twisted into a wry grin. "Of course. Speaking of your little friend, he should be here any minute."

My mouth fell open. "No! You didn't!"

Tom smirked. "I *did*. I need to make sure you lay low today, naughty girl. I need you out of sight and out of the mind of this Detective Stanley guy. From what I hear, he practically foams rabid at the mention of your name."

I scowled. "All I did was –"

Tom took me by the shoulders. "Val, listen to me. No more tricks. No more stakeouts. No more of your amateur investigation stuff. You're in seriously hot water. And I hate to break it to you, but 'Valiant Stranger' doesn't have the greatest powers of perception."

"But –"

Tom wrapped me in his arms. "Just stay out of trouble today. Promise me?"

I would have promised Tom if I could have. But I never went looking for trouble. It always seemed to find me all on its own.

"SO YOU REALLY LIKE the jewelry biz, huh?" I asked as Winky hauled in his box of fishing tackle and plopped it on the kitchen counter.

"Beats cremating critters, that's for sure. What's Tommy Boy up to today?"

"He's gonna check on the results of the license plates he gave his friend at the DMV. He's also going down to Sarasota. He wants to get a hold of that guy Bill Robo's employment application from the resort."

"Employment application. Now that's a sight I hope to never see again."

I poured a mug of coffee for Winky as he set up his mobile jewelry factory on the kitchen counter. "So, how much did it cost to get into this business? All the tackle and stuff?"

"Not that much. Old Joe at the Bait and Tackle Shack lets us have first crack at all his clearance stuff. Lets us buy the other stuff wholesale, too."

"That's cool. You know, you sound like a real businessman, Winky."

Winky slurped his coffee. "Why shore I do. What else would I sound like?"

I'd treaded close to his redneck toes, so I changed the subject. "I hear Milly and Vance are thinking about going to Hawaii for their honeymoon."

"Yep. Now me, personally? I wouldn't want to go there myself."

"Why not?"

"It's way across the Specific Ocean, ain't it?"

"Uh, yeah. So?"

"I don't trust all that water."

"But I thought you liked to fish."

"Yeah. From the shore."

My cellphone chirped with another text. I figured it was from Finkerman, and almost ignored it. But I thought again and hobbled over to the couch. I grabbed the phone from the coffee table. When I read the message, my knees buckled. I sat down on the sofa with a thud.

"I think I'll go lay down," I said to Winky.

He looked up from his tackle. "You look like a vampire done sucked all the blood outta ya. You need help?"

"No. I'll manage." I hobbled with the cane to my bedroom and sat on the edge of the bed. My fingers trembled so badly I could barely make out the message as I read it again.

"Having a blast with Bill." It wasn't the words, but the picture that accompanied it that had drained the blood from my face. In full color on my cellphone display was a photo of Cold Cuts from the shoulders up. Her neck had been slit from ear to ear.

Nooooo!!!!!

The walls of my bedroom suddenly folded in on me. My body boiled with pent-up rage. I wanted to scream and run as fast as I could from here to California. I wanted to punch Bill Robo in the face. But, oddly, I didn't want to cry. I wanted to be Valliant Stranger.

I wanted to live up to my name.

Fueled on by thoughts of revenge, I yanked up the window pane, pushed out the screen, and hobbled as fast as I could over to Shabby Maggie. As I turned the ignition and peeled down the driveway, this time I knew *exactly* where I was headed.

Valliant Stranger didn't have a driver's license or a credit card, but she had twenty bucks, a cellphone and enough determination to get where she was going, even if Maggie was belching blue smoke and sucking gas faster than a wino in a swimming pool full of Merlot.

Chapter Twenty-Five

I screeched into the parking lot by the entryway to the Pinellas County Morgue. I hesitated a moment, trying to decide whether to go it alone or call Tom. Deep down, I knew I should call him. But old habits die hard – especially when you're running on blind panic.

"Valiant Stranger!" a voice called out. I looked up from chewing off a fingernail. A slim man with a devilish goatee was strolling down the sidewalk in my direction, a huge paper cup of coffee in his hand.

I spit my chewed nail onto the asphalt. "Darren Dudley! I was just on my way to see you!"

"Well, it's my lucky day, then," the handsome coroner's clerk said. "I didn't think I'd ever see *you* again." He looked Shabby Maggie up and down and whistled. "Nice bat-mobile, Super Chick!"

I forgot about my sprained ankle and tried to get out of the car. It reminded me again. "Ouch!"

"You okay?"

"Yeah...just...never mind. Listen, Darren, I don't have a lot of time to chat. I need your help. Have you gotten any new bodies in the morgue in the last three days?"

Darren shot me a curious grin. "Should I bother to ask why?"

My eyebrows met in the middle of my forehead. "I'm looking for someone. Thirty-something. Caucasian. Female. Slim build."

"That makes two of us," Darren winked.

"I'm serious. A friend of mine is missing. Kidnapped...or...worse."

Darren's grin faded. "Oh. Well, come to think of it, I *do* have a body that could fit that description."

My gut fell to my knees. "Look. I just got this text and picture from her. Can you tell me if it's her?"

As I punched the message up on my cellphone, Darren came and stood beside the passenger door. He took the phone and studied the picture for a moment. "This can't be her," he said.

"Are you sure?"

"Yes. Ruby's got blue eyes and a nose piercing."

"Ruby?"

"Oh," Darren laughed. "You know me. That's what I nicknamed the stiff. Her nose piercing is a ruby. And she's kinda ugly, while your friend here is *hot.*"

"That's rude even for *you*, Darren. How can you say that? My friend is dead!" I burst into tears.

"Now hold on there, Super Girl," Darren said, his tone softening. "She's not dead. That's stage blood."

"What?" I said, and looked up from my steering wheel.

"And see here?" Darren poked at the screenshot. "Her eyes are glistening. Dead eyes don't do that."

"Are you sure? I mean, *one hundred percent* sure, Darren?"

"Yep. But even if I wasn't, there's one *dead* giveaway." Darren grinned mischievously. When I didn't react, he scrunched his nose and shrugged apologetically. "Sorry, I told you before, working here's made me...uh...*oblivious to subtlety.*"

I sniffed back a tear. "It's okay. So what makes you sure she's alive?"

"This picture is dated from last Halloween."

Hope leapt in my heart like a frisky bullfrog. I grabbed the phone from Darren. "What? Really?" I looked at the date. "But why would she send me *this* picture when she's missing –"

"Is she a bit of a prankster?" Darren asked.

"Huh?"

"Did she maybe go as a zombie last Halloween? It was a pretty popular theme."

"I don't know." I stared at the horrific image of Cold Cuts again.

I don't know whether to laugh that Cold Cuts is still alive, or kill her myself for putting me through this awful prank!

Suddenly, another thought swept away my hope. *Oh my word! Maybe it wasn't her prank. Maybe that crazy fisherman guy sent this. Maybe he was just toying with me, and Cold Cuts really was dead.*

"You okay?" Darren asked, interrupting my mental meltdown. "You look, I dunno. *Devastated.* You need me to drive you home?"

"Huh? Oh. No thanks, Darren. I really appreciate your help. I...I just need a moment."

"What's your friend's name?" Darren asked.

I looked up from the picture forlornly. "Cold Cuts."

Darren shot me a sarcastic face. "You're kidding."

When I didn't react, he backtracked. "Sorry. Listen, I hope she's all right." He took the phone from my hand and punched some numbers in it.

"I created a group text line with my number, yours and Cold Cuts," he said, handing me back the phone. "That way, if any more photos come in, I can take a look and let you know. Okay?"

"Okay," I muttered absently.

He shrugged apologetically. "Listen, I've got to get back to work. I was just on a coffee break."

"Yeah. Thanks."

I watched Darren disappear behind the doors to the county morgue, then turned the ignition on Maggie. She rattled and coughed a cloud of grey smoke. I prayed that both she and Cold Cuts would somehow hold together long enough to make it back home.

I PULLED UP TO MY HOUSE and groaned. Tom's SUV was in the driveway. I'd been caught going AWOL again. *Crap on a cracker!* For a second I wished it had been Finkerman's yellow Hummer instead. What could I say to Tom that would make this right? I'd gone and broken all the rules he'd laid out just a couple of hours ago.

It was official. I really *was* a horrible fiancé.

I turned off the ignition and tried to brace myself for Tom's wrath. I was still reeling with shock from the picture of Cold Cuts and the mixed bag of news from Darren. I knew if Tom was in the mood for an argument, it wouldn't take much to make me crack. As I reached to open my car door, the front door of my house flew open. Tom glared at me and I froze in place. The cold, hard look on his face confirmed my suspicions. He was totally pissed.

"Did you have any luck with Monty?" I asked as he marched up to the car. My attempt to break the ice didn't even make a mark in it.

"No. I never had the chance," Tom forced between pursed lips. He jerked the handle on my car door and yanked it open. "Couldn't stay put for *two measly hours*. Where *were* you?"

Goober ambled toward us, instigating a temporary détente. "Well, there she is, Ms. Slippery Snake herself." He looked me up and down, and smoothed his caterpillar moustache with a thumb and forefinger. He patted Tom on the back. "Looks like she's back all safe and sound, Tom. I'll take my leave now and escape the nuclear fallout."

"Bye, Goober," I called after him as he walked down the driveway. I turned to face Tom. He was glaring at me, hopping mad. "Tom –" I began, but didn't get any further.

"Save it for the ride to Sarasota," Tom hissed. He offered a hand to help me onto my feet.

"Sarasota?"

"Yes." Tom helped me to his SUV and opened the door. "I was on the phone with my contact at the Sarasota police station. Apparently, someone ratted us out to Detective Stanley. He cut in on the line while we were talking and ripped me a new one for sticking my nose in his business. Then he suggested for my own sake that I make myself useful and bring you back in for questioning."

"Why? I've already told him everything I know. Has something changed?"

"Yes."

Tom held my cane as I scrambled into the passenger seat.

"What?"

Tom blew out a breath. "Val, they found a body. And it fits Cold Cuts' description."

THE COLD WAR BETWEEN Tom and me continued all the way across the Sunshine Skyway Bridge to the Sarasota County line. Finally, I couldn't take the silence any longer.

"Tom, the reason I went out –"

"Val, I don't want to hear it right now," Tom barked. His eyes never wavered from the road ahead. "All I asked you to do was take it easy for a couple of hours. But no. That was too much to ask."

"Tom –"

"I said I don't want to hear it."

"Well you're going to!" I screeched. "I got a text from Cold Cuts!"

Tom nearly wrecked the SUV. "Why didn't you tell –"

"I *tried!*"

Tom glanced my way, his cold expression melting slightly. "Okay, okay. What did she say?"

"Having a blast with Bill."

"What? So...so she's all right?"

"That's just it. I don't know. There was a picture with the text. Of Cold Cuts. With her throat slit."

"What?"

"But it wasn't real," I added quickly. "I mean, it was taken on Halloween or something. The guy at the morgue said she was alive. At least in *that* picture, anyway."

"The guy at the...?" Tom began. Then shook his head. "Never mind. Why would she do that?"

"That's what I've been trying to figure out. Was it a joke by Cold Cuts? If so, why wouldn't she just say so? The only thing that makes sense...Tom, what if it was some kind of sick threat from that psycho fisherman?"

Tom bit his lip. "You tried calling her back?"

"No. I wanted to wait...and talk to *you* first."

"Oh." What remained of Tom's anger evaporated in the seriousness of the moment. He reached over and squeezed my hand.

"Should I call her, Tom? What if the psycho picks up?"

"No. Wait. We'll do it when we get to Sarasota. A few more minutes won't matter."

"Okay. Look, I'm sorry if –"

"It's okay, Val. Given the circumstances, I would have done the same thing."

A sigh of relief escaped my tight lungs. I gave Tom's hand a squeeze and sniffed back a tear. "Did you have any luck with the license plates?"

"Not sure yet. Most checked out. But there were a couple of odd ones worth following up on." Tom turned off the highway and stopped at a light. He looked at me, his face dead serious. "Val, when we get there, we'll need to give Detective Stanley everything we've got. It's his case to work, whether we like it or not. Being charged with obstruction of justice would not be good for you. And it wouldn't help *my career*, either."

"Okay. You have my word."

A couple of blocks later, Tom pulled into the parking lot of the Sarasota Police Station. "You ready?" he asked.

I nodded.

He took my phone, punched speed dial for Cold Cuts and put it on speaker. We sat in the cab of his SUV and listened to the phone ring. It rang and rang and rang. Finally, Tom clicked the phone off and handed it back to me.

"At this point, maybe no news is good news," he said.

"Sure," I said.

But neither one of us believed it.

Chapter Twenty-Six

"Whatever they tell you, try to act surprised, even if you know it already," Tom said as he helped me hobble across the parking lot toward the main entrance of the Sarasota Police Station. "At this point, Stanley may try to shock you into a confession. You're not supposed to know about the body part being sea pork – or the blood in the bathroom being chemicals."

"Okay," I said. "I'll do my best."

Tom kissed me, gave me a hug and opened the door. As soon as I set foot in the place, we were pounced on by an angry, red-faced Detective James Stanley.

"I'm glad to see you can follow *some* orders," he hissed at Tom. "This way, Ms. Fremden." He grabbed my arm with his sausage fingers and tugged me toward the interrogation room. I locked eyes with Tom for one last second. The helplessness that had begun to snarl my mind fell away. Tom's eyes glowed with the subtle strength of knowing that, no matter what anyone else thought, *we* were in the right.

I SHIFTED MY BUTT ON the chair and wondered for a second why they called it a 'hot seat.' The interrogation room was freezing, and the hard, metal chair I sat in was as cold and sticky as a dirty frog's bottom.

"This is not looking good for you, Ms. Fremden," Detective Stanley sneered. He chortled mildly, causing the blubbery folds that hung like meat curtains between his chin and chest to wobble grotesquely. "As you know, Ms. Piddle has been missing three days now."

"It's Piddle*ton*," I said, trying to be helpful. "And she's probably been missing for *four* days."

I guess Detective Stanley didn't like being helped.

"I *said* Piddleton," he barked in my face. "And today is Wednesday. She's been missing since Monday. That's three days, according to my basic math calculations."

"Yes sir," I backtracked, for Tom's sake. "What I meant was, I'm beginning to think that it wasn't Cold – Ms. Piddleton in the bed next to mine that Monday morning."

Detective Stanley's brow furrowed below his dead-squirrel toupee. "Why would you think that?"

"I'd rather not say."

He looked at me sourly. "I'd rather you *did*."

"Well...the person in the bed was *snoring*. My friend Goober told me she doesn't snore."

The detective's face grew as dull as wax. "Goober?"

"Uh...his real name is Gerald...something or other."

"You know, your disrespect for me and this investigation is getting pretty tiresome, Ms. Fremden. Maybe this will get you to take it more seriously."

Detective Stanley pulled a photo from a folder. He slid the picture across the table toward me. It was the face of a dead woman, her mouth open, dull eyes staring blankly. "She was found yesterday."

"That's not Cold Cuts. I mean, *Ms. Piddleton*. That's *Ruby*," I said, recognizing the nose piercing Darren had described.

Detective Stanley's cruel smile came unglued and fell off his face. "You killed *her*, too?"

"What? No! I heard about her...at the morgue. In St. Petersburg."

"And tell me, what were you doing at the morgue?"

"I was checking to see if, you know, Ms. Piddleton was there."

"That, Ms. Fremden, is a very odd thing for a person to do."

"I know it looks weird. But this morning, I got a text message from her and –"

"And you didn't think to tell us?" Detective Stanley bellowed. His fist hit the table with a thud that reverberated around the small, concrete box of a room.

"I'm telling you *now*, if you'll let me!"

The detective bit his fat lip and took a deep breath. "All right. Continue. What did the message say?"

"'Having a blast with Bill.' But it came with a picture of Cold Cuts with her throat slit. I didn't want to believe it. I was in shock. So I took it to my friend at the morgue."

"Of course," he said sourly. "Everyone has a friend at the morgue nowadays."

"Look, just for the record, Darren said it was an old photo. From Halloween. So I didn't think –"

"That's just *it*, Fremden," Detective Stanley said, his condescending tone rising again. "You *didn't* think. Give me your phone."

I handed it over. "'Having a blast with Bill,'" he mumbled aloud. He stared at the picture. "Tell me, how long have you known Bill Robo?" His eyes shifted quickly from the phone to my face.

"I'd never seen him before I took that yoga class at the resort."

"And your friend Cold – Ms. Pid – oh, hell! *Cold Cuts*. How long has she known Robo?"

"The same."

"She just met him as well. Tell me. Do you think she would have voluntarily gone off with him?"

"I...I don't know. Maybe. They were...um...*intimate*. When we got caught in a storm on Dog Island."

Detective Stanley's face reddened. "And you didn't think this was relevant information?"

"He seemed like a nice guy...."

"The guy could be a murderer, for all you know!" Detective Stanley barked.

I flinched. "I know, now. But at the time...he didn't seem like the type to...." I looked for reassurance in the detective's eyes. I didn't get it.

He pursed his lips and spat his next words. "Nobody ever *seems* like the type, Ms. Fremden. Until they *are*. You saw the blood all over the place."

"But it wasn't blood!"

The detective's angry eyes shifted with surprise. "How would you know that?"

"I...I don't! I just meant, I *hope* it's not blood. I want my friend to be *alive*, Detective Stanley. I *love* her!"

"Love, huh?" the detective sneered. "You've got a funny way of showing it. I see, now. This is this some kind of love triangle gone bad, isn't it? The desk clerk seemed to think you and your friend were quite chummy. On holiday together in the honeymoon suite. Then this Bill Robo character comes in and screws everything up. Well, now. That just wouldn't do. So you took care of the both of them!"

He pounded his fist on the table so hard I nearly fell out of my chair.

"No!" I cried out, more angry than afraid. "That's *not* what happened. Me and Cold Cuts...it was all *a joke*. A *misunderstanding* we took it too far. I was supposed to be there with my boyfriend, Tom. He couldn't make it the first day –"

"How convenient," Detective Stanley snarled. "Listen, I'll come clean with you if you come clean with me."

"What do you mean?"

"That body part that washed up on the beach? It turned out to be sea chops."

"Sea pork," I began, but the surprise and suspicion on the detective's face reminded me I wasn't supposed to know. "I...uh...sea pork chops? You say?"

"Not pork chops. *Sea* chops. It's some kind a bull crap that lives on the reefs. Anyway, all that blood in the bathroom. Turns out it's chemicals. Bleach and ammonia. Could have been used for cleanup." Detective Stanley paused and waited for my reaction.

"You don't say," I offered.

"Then there's the pliers and the tooth. Open your mouth, Ms. Fremden."

I started to object, then gave in and did as instructed.

"Wider. So I can see your molars."

I opened wider.

"I see you've got all of yours. How convenient."

"What do you mean?"

"It's not illegal to pull your own tooth in these United States. But practicing dentistry without a license *is*."

"I see," I said.

"That leaves the blood trail from the cottage to the beach."

"But I thought it was fish...*fishy*, Detective." *Oh crap!* "Back to the tooth. I mean...why would someone pull their tooth...*on vacation at the beach?* If you could afford that fancy resort, you could afford a dentist, right?"

"You've obviously have never needed a root canal, Ms. Fremden."

"No," I admitted.

Detective Stanley blew out a breath. "The facts still remain. Your so-called *friend* is missing, along with Bill Robo. No one's heard a word from either of them."

"But what about the text message I showed you?"

Detective Stanley's overblown confidence missed a beat. "I meant *until now*. Besides, we don't know if she sent it. It could have come from whoever knows where she is, and what's happened to her. It could have come from *you*."

"But...but I couldn't have sent this message to myself!"

"Sure you could have," Detective Stanley sneered. "Easy. You just used her phone after you did her in."

"HOW'D IT GO?" TOM ASKED as he climbed out of his SUV. He'd waited for me outside the station, and stayed in his vehicle to avoid rubbing any more cop elbows the wrong way.

"The body turned out to be Ruby instead of Cold Cuts, so Detective Stanley was forced to let me go," I explained as Tom helped me crawl into the passenger seat. "But he'd made it crystal clear I wasn't off the hook."

"I bet he did."

"At least I got my purse back," I said, and grabbed the cane from Tom. "You know, Detective Stanley told me not to leave my residence or he'd have me arrested. Can he do that?"

"Not really," Tom said, as he scooted onto the driver's seat and shut his door. He turned the ignition on the silver 4Runner. "It's an old cop trick. But some people still fall for it."

I scowled. "He told me to stop playing Miss Marple and let him do his job."

Tom smiled wryly. "I've told you the same thing. Not that it's done any good."

"This morning, you said you didn't have a chance to talk to Monty, the desk clerk at the resort."

"Right." Tom reversed and pulled out of the parking spot.

"Well, we're here in Sarasota. We might as well stop by and give it a go."

Tom hit the brakes. "Have you not heard a word I've said, Val? I can't get involved anymore. I *told* you that."

"Okay, okay!" I snapped. "But I need to stop by there anyway."

Tom shifted into forward. "What for?"

"I want to see if they still have my gold thong bikini."

162 of MARGARET LASHLEY

He laughed bitterly and hit the gas. "Sure you do."

"Tom, I think Monty has it out for me."

"Why do you say that?"

"I can just feel it. You know. That gut reaction you're always talking about. I just know it."

"Val, there's *no way* you're talking me into taking you to see Monty."

"But –"

"Not for all the buts in Birmingham."

"Then what are you going to do now?"

"I'm taking you home, then I'm going back to work. There's no point wasting a whole week's vacation spinning our wheels like this."

Chapter Twenty-Seven

Tom dropped me off at my house, but not before making sure my next-door neighbor Laverne was home to keep an eye on me. I was angry at Tom for giving up on the case. I was in no mood for company – much less a dose of Laverne's silly optimism.

No sooner had Tom's SUV disappeared out the driveway when the doorbell rang. I was hoping against odds for Finkerman. At least then I could punch someone in the nose. But it was Laverne. I groaned, opened the door, and braced myself for a tidal wave of empty-headed good cheer.

"Hi, Laverne."

"It's all my fault!" the old woman screeched, and burst into tears.

"What? Come in here. What are you talking about, Laverne?"

"It's *my* fault, Val, honey. The first time I saw it, I had a bad feeling. I knew it and I didn't warn you!"

"Warn me about what?"

"*The curse of Vendaygo!*" Laverne sobbed, and grabbed a hold of me like a starving leech.

She wept on my shoulder until her mascara streamed in twin black torrents down the front of my shirt. I always knew Laverne was loopy, but *a curse?* She'd just flown up the crazy-old-lady scale to a whole new level. My father Justas had a saying for folks who believed in voodoo and curses. "Their cornbread ain't done in the middle."

"Have a seat," I said, and peeled Laverne off me. "Let me get you something to drink, then I want you to tell me all about this curse thing."

I hobbled to the kitchen as Laverne flopped into my easy chair. "Vendaygo," Laverne sniffed. "The curse of Vendaygo, Val. I gave it to you!"

Laverne burst into tears again. I was going to fix her a glass of tea, but switched to gin and tonic instead. "Curse? Come on, Laverne. You don't really believe that, do you?"

"I never did...until it happened to *me*."

"What are you talking about?" I handed her a drink and sat down on the couch. She took a big gulp of booze and spilled her story like a crook hanging by the ankle out a thirty-story window.

"When I was working as a cabaret dancer at the Flamingo, this guy Vinnie Vendaygo was sweet on me. But I wasn't too keen on him." She looked over at me.

"Okay."

"Well, my best friend Donna told me to give him a chance. I already knew deep down in my heart that Vinnie wasn't right guy for me, but I let him think he was. He took me to the movies and dinner, and some fancy shows. We were having a good time until one night, he up and surprised me with a ring. He said it wasn't an engagement ring, just something to let the world know I was his girl."

"What's so bad about that?"

Laverne stared at me for a moment with her melted raccoon eyes. "Nothing. On *his* part. But for me, it all felt like a big, ugly lie. I shouldn't have taken the ring, Val. But I did. I wore it home that night feeling like a fraud. I couldn't sleep. I made my mind up I'd give it back to him the next day, but he went and got run over by a bus before I had the chance!" Laverne shook her head in sorrow. "I should have realized it then. But I didn't. It took me way too long to put two and two together."

"What do you mean?"

"The ring was *cursed*, Val. From then on out, every time I wore it, something awful would happen. I'd get let go from my job. I'd rip a pair of stockings. I'd lose my keys to my apartment. Horrible things like that!"

"They don't seem out of the –"

"So I stopped wearing it and shoved it in a drawer!" Laverne lamented. "I hadn't thought about that ring for *years*. Then last year, I found it in a drawer. I tell you Val, it was like finding a rattlesnake curled up and ready to strike!"

"What did you do?"

"I got out my oven mitts, picked it up and threw it in the trash."

"So, the curse is over, Laverne. How could you give it to me?"

"Remember when you came back from your mom's all sick, and I made you that soup?"

"Yes."

"When I saw your ring, my heart nearly stopped. It looked just like the blue sapphire ring Vinnie had given me. But then I read the inscription in the band, and I figured it couldn't be. You see, mine was inscribed, too. But with just one big, loopy L on it...for Laverne, you know?"

"Yes," I said, and almost rolled my eyes from the irony. "A big loopy L for Laverne."

"Take your ring off, Val, and look at inscription. That L in Luv. It's loopy, just like the L on the ring Vinnie Vendaygo gave me."

"What?" I took the ring off and studied the L. It was an entirely different font than the other letters. "But...Laverne, even if it *is* the same ring, how could Tom end up with it?"

"I don't know. But I'm sure of one thing. You've got the curse, now, Val. What happened to Cold Cuts.... And you getting accused of murdering her. It's *all my fault!* I should have thrown that blasted ring in the ocean – or buried in the dirt!"

"Laverne, it's *not* your fault," I said. "You know I've *always* had bad luck. But if it makes you feel better, I'll take the ring off."

Laverne's face brightened a little as I slipped the ring from my finger and set it on the coffee table beside my cellphone. As if on cue, the phone buzzed. I looked at the display. "Unknown Caller." I looked back at Laverne. She was staring at me like a lost soul in need of forgiveness.

"Laverne, could you do me a favor?"

She sprang at the chance. "Anything, honey!"

"I have a headache. Could you get me a tablet from the medicine cabinet?"

"Sure thing, sugar."

"While you're in there, take a moment for yourself. You look like you just lost a game of Maybelline paintball."

Laverne laughed softly, and clomped off toward the bathroom. I smashed the answer button on my phone and slammed it to my ear.

"Hello? Are you still there?"

"One of our operatives spotted the RV in Key Largo," said the voice of Bernard Charles.

"Oh my lor! Is my friend Cold Cuts okay?"

"We don't have enough information to say at this point. Our operative noticed a man in a '60s-era Winnebago who fit the profile you gave us for Bill Robo. He wasn't able to see the plates, but the suspect was driving the vehicle down Highway 1, accompanied by a redheaded, Caucasian female of indeterminate age. Unfortunately, at that point, the agent ran out of fuel and had to pull over to the side of the road."

"Oh."

"You said Ms. Piddleton was brunette, correct?"

"Yes. But that RV...it's full of...*disguises.*"

"What do you mean?

"Cold Cuts – I mean Ms. Piddleton – she works on movie sets. She travels around with all kinds of wigs and costumes in the RV. It could have been her in a red wig. She's got a million of them stowed in the RV. Everything from toupees to merkins."

"What's a merkin?"

"Um...maybe you should google it." My confidence in my unknown ally skipped a beat. I'd thought that Mr. Charles knew *everything*.

"I see. Any other news we should be aware of?"

"I got a text message from Ms. Piddleton."

"When?"

"This morning. I was going to call you but –"

"What did she say?"

"That's just it. I'm not sure if it was really from her. It was a text. It said, 'Having a blast with Bill.' That doesn't sound like something she'd really say, you know? It came with a picture of her looking like her throat was slashed. But the photo was dated last Halloween. So the whole thing could have been a prank."

"Or a taunt," Mr. Charles said.

"What do you mean?"

"Well, I didn't want to bring this up unless it became relevant. But the name Bill Robo is definitely an alias."

"Are you sure?"

"Yes. We haven't been able to track down anything on him. That means he's either got no criminal record, or he's slick enough to have never been caught."

I gulped. "Which one do you think it is?"

"In my line of work, an honest man doesn't need an alias."

"Oh."

"Sorry I don't have anything more substantial to tell you at this time. I'll be in touch."

The phone went to dial tone. I listened to it until Laverne's voice broke my blank stare.

"Who was that, honey?"

"Oh." I clicked off the phone. "A friend."

"That's nice. Here's your tablet," Laverne said, and handed me a Tums.

"Thanks, Laverne, but I meant the pain pills in the blue bottle."

I started to get up, but Laverne wasn't having it. "You stay put, sugar. I'll get it. What is it with you and blue, anyway?"

"What do you meant?"

"Blue Ty D Bol, blue Nyquil, blue bottles. You've got a thing for blue colored stuff, don't you?"

A couple of cells fired in my brain. "Oh my...," I began. "I think I know what happened in the bathroom!"

Laverne flinched and jumped back. "Whatever it was, I swear I didn't do it!"

Chapter Twenty-Eight

When Tom arrived at my place that evening, I was chomping at the bit to tell him what I'd figured out. Maybe *then* he'd believe in my investigative talents. I figured a beer wouldn't hurt anything either.

"Hey, how was your day?" I asked as he came through the door. "Ready for a beer?"

"Hey." He watched me hobble over to him on my cane. "What are you doing on your feet?"

"I've been taking it easy. My ankle's feeling a lot better."

"Glad to hear it." Tom took the beer and collapsed onto the couch. "Sorry to say, but I've got no more news on Cold Cuts."

I sat beside him. "Me either. But I've got a theory."

Tom shot me a dubious look. "Uh oh."

I shoved him on the shoulder. "I wish you'd take me seriously. I think I've figured out an important clue."

"What is it?"

"All those chemicals in the bathroom? The ones that looked like blood?"

"Yeah."

"I think it could be hair dye."

Tom nearly choked on his beer. "Hair dye?"

"Yes. I got a call from Bernard Charles today. He told me his team thinks they spotted the RV in the Keys. A man who fit Bill Robo's description was driving. He was accompanied by a red-headed woman."

"And?"

"Don't you see? Cold Cuts dyed her hair in the bathroom sink."

"Huh," Tom said, and contemplated the label on his beer. "That's a possibility. But why was the dye all over the place, then? I mean, it was on the ceiling and *everywhere.*"

"I don't know. Maybe someone...*interrupted her* when she was doing it."

"Maybe. Or it could be that the perpetrator colored her hair. To disguise her identity after...well, you know."

"Crap. I was hoping this would make things clearer. It's just made them worse."

"It's a clue, Val. And a good one. What made you think of it?"

"Something Laverne said. About my penchant for Ty D Bol."

"Huh?"

"The blue dye in it. Something just clicked in my brain."

"Leave it to Laverne." Tom noticed the ring on the coffee table and picked it up. "Why aren't you wearing this?"

"Oh. Because it upset Laverne."

"What do you mean?"

"She has it in her head that the ring is cursed."

"Cursed?"

"Yeah." I bit my lip. "She thinks it's the same ring she threw away last year. Some guy named Vinnie had given it to her, then got hit by a bus. Every time she wore it, she had bad luck."

"Why does she think it's the same ring?"

"Because of the loopy L in Luv. Where did you get the ring, anyway?"

"I found it in the middle of the road about a block from here."

My jaw fell open. "So Laverne was right. It probably *is* the same ring."

"Odds are, yes."

I pouted angrily. "So why did you give it to *me* for an engagement ring?"

"Don't give me that look," Tom said. "It wasn't that I was trying to be cheap."

"Then what?"

"The day I found it, I'd been thinking about asking you to marry me. I saw a glint in the road and stopped to see what it was. I found the ring. It was beautiful. I'd taken it as a sign of good luck. That we were meant to be together."

I crinkled my nose, unconvinced. "Well, there's an ironic twist if I ever saw one."

Tom looked hurt. "What do you mean?"

"I see it as just the opposite. I think it's a sign that our relationship is *cursed*, Tom. That maybe we *aren't* meant to be together."

Tom's eyes grew wide with shock. "What?"

"Maybe you should leave."

"You're kidding."

"No. I'm not."

"That does it!" Tom snapped, and slammed his beer bottle down on the coffee table. "Val, you run so hot and cold, I never know if I'm gonna be scalded alive or frozen to death by you!"

He jerked to his feet and stomped to the door. "I've had it. I can't take it anymore." He opened the door, took a step out. Then he turned to face me one last time. "Make up your mind what you want once and for all, Val. Or don't ever call me ever again."

A FEW MINUTES AFTER Tom left, my cellphone buzzed. My heart leapt in my throat. I clicked to answer it. "I'm sorry!" I cried out. "I don't know what I was thinking!"

"A confession at last," Finkerman's slimy voice said in victory.

Something inside me boiled over and screamed. I clicked off the phone and flung it across the room. Then I limped to the kitchen and poured myself a gin and tonic – with way more gin than tonic.

Chapter Twenty-Nine

I'd finally gone and done it. I'd pushed Tom to the edge of the cliff. Maybe even over it. I'd slept about an hour last night, give or take forty-five minutes. I was delirious. I must have been. I'd actually called Winky and asked for his help. Maggie had been belching blue smoke, and I needed to get to Sarasota.

I'd had all night to think about the disaster my life was in, but Cold Cuts trumped my own problems at the moment. I went over the details in my mind again, searching for anything I might have missed:

When I'd woken up Monday morning in the cottage, someone was in the bed beside mine. I was sure of that, because of the snoring. I'd gone into the bathroom. At that point, it was clean – there was nothing amiss. If someone did *dye their hair in the sink at the cottage, they had to have done it after I left the room at 5:30 a.m.*

I'd gone for a walk on the beach and read until around 8:45 a.m. Then I'd peeked my head in the room to see if Cold Cuts wanted to go to breakfast. It looked as if she were still asleep in bed, but maybe not. It could have just been bunched up covers. She could have been in the bathroom instead. I strained my brain, trying to remember if I'd heard snoring that time or not. I just couldn't be certain. And I hadn't checked the bathroom, either.

Monty was in the lobby before 9 a.m., because he led me to the breakfast room, where Detective Stanley was making waffles in his dead-squirrel toupee. I'd left and run into Brad at the beach, then headed to Doug's

Dugout for breakfast, but got body slammed, then chased back to the room by the tornado. All of that happened within an hour. So whatever happened in the bathroom, and to Cold Cuts, had to have taken place between 5:30 and 10:00 in the morning.

Coffee was already available in the breakfast room at half-past five, so someone had to be up and about by then. Brad or Monty or someone else? Either way, people were up and about when Cold Cuts went missing. Someone had to have seen something. *I needed to get back to the resort to find out who.*

I'd shared my thoughts with Winky while he was bent over Maggie's engine. He looked up, wiped more grease on his face, and said, "Well, you ain't goin' nowheres in this *here* vehicle."

"Why not? What's wrong?"

"You need a new set of rings."

The word "rings" echoed in my ears. I pushed the image of a blue sapphire out of my mind.

"Do you think the Dodge can make it?" I asked, and nodded toward his rusty, faded-blue van.

"Shore. She ain't much to look at, but she's got a heart of gold."

"YOU DON'T MIND IF WE stop at Old Joe's Bait and Tackle Shack, do you?" Winky asked as he pulled onto Gulf Boulevard heading south. "It's just over yonder on Sunset Beach by Caddy's."

"That's fine," I said. "I guess the Playing Hooky jewelry business is doing pretty well."

"Yep. I got to restock the earring racks for the second time this week. They's all out a yore favorite ones again. You know, them with the hard-bodied grubs."

"Nice." I tried to be enthusiastic, but no sleep and no Tom had sapped me dry of it.

Winky took a right off Gulf onto the narrow road that paralleled Sunset Beach. Old Joe's wasn't much more than a shack, but it benefited from the draw its neighbor, Caddy's beach bar, had on tourists and locals alike.

"There's ol' Joe hisself," Winky said as he parked by the wooden hut no bigger than a dilapidated garage. In the open door frame stood a skinny old man who looked to be comprised mostly of a tanned leather hide and a shaggy grey beard. He waved a boney hand of welcome.

We piled out of the Dodge van. I grabbed my cane and I limped behind Winky up to the shack. "There's my feller," said Old Joe. "This your girlfriend?"

"Lord, no!" Winky said in a tone that did nothing to bolster my self-esteem.

"Hi, I'm Joe," the old man said, and extended a hand the color and texture of a baseball glove.

"Val," I said. "Nice place you've got here."

It was a polite formality. The narrow aisles in the run-down shack were crammed with an odd, dusty assortment of junk that appeared to have been abandoned to time and neglect. Tourist beach necessities like sunscreen, floats and kites were mixed in amongst a tangled heap of fishing rods, ridiculous looking rubber lures and a bubbling old fish tank full of algae and live bait shrimp. Why anyone would willingly sacrifice a perfectly good, tasty shrimp on the odd chance to catching a fish, I'd never understand.

"Got your earrings right here," Winky said, and opened his tackle box up by the antique cash register.

"Good!" Old Joe said. "Let me pay you what I owe you."

While the two men hashed out their high-roller finances, I poked around the place. An old wooden sign that read, "Fishermen know all the right holes," made me smile. I thumped along toward the fish tank and spotted a set of opaque shot glasses featuring a big-bosomed woman in a bikini. Instructions read, "Add booze and watch her bikini disappear!" *No thanks.*

I peered into the fish tank and watched the shrimp jet around, doing whatever shrimp do. Next to the tank was a pile of egg crates. Curious, I picked one up and opened it. Ten thousand crickets inside it all jumped in my face at once.

"Aaarrghh!" I screamed. I lost my balance and flung the egg carton as far as I could on my way to a hard landing on the filthy concrete floor. On the way down, my cane managed to take out a half-dozen fishing rods. They toppled onto me as the crickets hopped all over my body in search of a getaway.

"Gaul-dang it, Val!" Winky bellowed. He came over and offered me a hand. "You all right?"

"Not really," I muttered as he pulled me to standing. "But I'll live. I'm sorry about this, Old Joe. I'll pay for the crickets, and whatever else got destroyed."

Old Joe smiled the kind of happy-go-lucky smile I'd envied my entire life. "Don't you worry a jot, Miss Val. We all make mistakes now and then."

"Well, thank you," I said, feeling guilty. I wanted to buy something to make amends. I glanced around the shack. "I'll take a couple of those shot glasses over there."

Old Joe grinned and reached for the glasses. "Whatever floats your boat, young lady."

"SMOOTH MOVE, EX-LAX," Winky teased as we left the shack.

I opened the door of the Dodge and tossed my bag of shot glasses inside. I was about to climb in when I had a thought.

"Hey Winky. How about a beer at Caddy's? I owe you for the ride." The truth was, my *own* heart could use a little anesthetizing.

Winky grinned. "Let no man say I ever turned down the opportunity for a free beer."

We walked through the sand over to Caddy's beach bar. It wasn't much more than a shack either. Just bigger – with picnic tables in the sand and a rooftop deck. I ordered us a couple of beers and joined Winky at a stool by a clapped-together wooden railing overlooking the beach. The sun, blue sky and white sand almost made me forget my troubles. I clinked by bottle against his.

"To you and Winnie," I said.

Winky wagged his ginger eyebrows. "And to you and Tom."

My troubles returned. "Thanks."

Winky took a long draw off his beer, then hopped off his stool. "Headin' to the little boys' room." He jangled the keys to his van at me. "Try not to do nothin' else stupid 'til I get back."

I forced a smile, then turned my eyes toward the shoreline. *No more Tom. Cold Cuts was missing. What did I have to celebrate, anyway? Just the hope things wouldn't get any worse?*

Someone tapped me on the shoulder. I looked, but no one was there. Winky was playing a trick on me. I tried the other shoulder and nearly gagged on my beer. A tall, skinny, pasty white guy with a head full of frizzy red hair grinned at me like a mummified skull in a carnival freak show.

"Hi there," Ferrol Finkerman said. "Having a nice day?"

"What are *you* doing here?" I snarled.

"I came to see you, of course."

"But...how did you know I was here?"

"You have your habits, and I have my spies," Finkerman said with the evil, condescending pleasure of a cartoon bad guy.

"Who's your spy?"

Finkerman shook his head as if I were a simpleton. "You really think I'd tell you?"

I blew out a breath. "I won't bother asking what you want, Finkerman."

"Good. Save us both the trouble." Finkerman handed me a sealed manila envelope. "Sign here that you received it. Then read 'em and weep. Assault with intention to humiliate. I'd say...hmmmm....fifteen grand ought to make my client feel better."

"Fifteen grand!"

Finkerman laughed at getting a rise out of me. "Has a nice ring to it, wouldn't you say?"

"I'll ring something all right!" Winky bellowed as he marched toward us. "Your neck! Finkerman, you rotten, bone-pickin' vulture!"

Winky put up his dukes for a fight. I wrapped my hands around his fists and pushed them down.

"Let it go, Winky," I said. "Before the vulture gets you, too."

I WAS FEELING PRETTY defeated when Winky turned the van back onto Gulf Boulevard and headed toward Sarasota. Something told me I was running out of time – in more ways than one.

"I just got to get some fuel, and we'll be on our way," Winky said solemnly. My doom and gloom had begun to infect him, too.

I sat in the car sullenly as he pumped the gas, my eyes avoiding the manila envelope in the seat beside me. My phone rang. The display read, "Unknown Caller." I snatched it up.

"Hello?"

"Here's the latest," Bernard Charles said. "The RV was spotted heading north on I-75 just outside of Naples."

"North? That's back toward the resort."

"Wouldn't be the first time a perpetrator returned to the scene of crime."

"So you think a real crime's been committed?"

"I'm afraid so. The blood on the pliers. There's no definite DNA match yet, but the type matches that of Ms. Piddleton. Have you heard anything else from her?"

"No not a word. We tried calling her, but no one picked up."

"Okay. I'll be in touch."

I clicked off the phone as Winky climbed in. "Woo doggy. I just priced a set of rings for Maggie. They's gonna set you back $78.39. Yore whole dang car ain't hardly worth that!"

I burst into tears.

Winky patted me on the back. "It's just money, Val. But seein's how you're in a state, I'm gonna turn us around and take you home. I'll get the parts and work on Maggie in the mornin'. Then we'll give Sarasota another try tomorrow. Okay?"

Who was I kidding? I couldn't help Cold Cuts. I couldn't even help myself.

"Okay," I sobbed. I buried my head in my hands and cried all the way back home.

Chapter Thirty

I woke up on the couch Friday morning with a broken neck and a pepperoni slice clinging to my cheek like a greasy kiss from an ugly stranger. It was 5:03 a.m. and Finkerman's lawsuit papers were scattered on top of me like a hobo's blanket. I turned my head slightly. Big mistake. I'd awoken the gin genie trapped inside my noggin. He started pounding to get out.

I lay dead still on the couch, contemplating whether it was worth the cost to move again to fetch a headache tablet. Yesterday came flooding back. *No word from Tom. The cricket attack. Finkerman's lawsuit. Cold Cuts' blood on the pliers.*

The doorbell rang and jarred another memory. Winky had promised to come over and fix Maggie.

The plan was for Winnie to drop him off before her morning shift at Davie's Donuts. I hadn't realized it would be *this* early. As I hauled myself to standing, the gin genie broke out a set of base drums and beat a throbbing riff in the space between my ears. I grabbed the cane and tentatively put weight on my left foot. It registered only mild discomfort, compared to my thumping head.

"You look like somethin' the cat dragged in," Winky said when I opened the door.

"Good morning to you, too," I grumbled. "Coffee?"

"Wouldn't mind a cup. You okay, there, Val Pal?"

"I've been worse. But I've been better, too," I muttered as I limped to the kitchen. "Thanks for coming over to work on Maggie. You still fixing people's cars on the side?"

"Sporatical, yeah. But I hear the real money nowadays is in mass marketin'."

"What do you mean?" I asked and fiddled with the stack of coffee filters, trying to free one from its death grip with the rest of the stack.

"Goober told me somethin' called 'social media' opened up a whole new way to make big money. He's workin' on getting' hisself a followin' on Snapchap, pestering folks."

"What? Why?"

"Said he read about a feller got paid off a couple million bucks just to stop bein' a pain in the hind end and leave them Snapchap folks alone. I reckon I could do that, myself."

I shook my head, immediately regretted it, and clicked the on button on the coffee machine. "You're always dreaming and scheming."

Winky smiled proudly and hooked a thumb in the armpit of the ragged hole in his t-shirt where a sleeve used to be. "Sure. Why not? The good Lord didn't make me this way for nothin'."

I sighed with envy. Winky was proud of who he was. I wished I could've said the same about myself. Here I was, fifty years old and still questioning my every move and motive. What was wrong with me? I pulled two mugs from the cupboard. "How long you think it'll take to get Maggie going again?"

"Less time than it'll take to fix you up, by the looks of it."

I hung my pounding head. "Yesterday was a rough day, Winky. You know, Tom and I broke up two days ago."

Winky let out a low whistle. "Gaul-dang it, Val. How come you never said nothin' about it yesterday?"

I shrugged and poured the coffee. "What could I say?"

"Uh...that you broke up with Tom?" Winky's eyes rolled around in his freckled face. "This ain't socket science, Val."

"Rocket."

"All right, then, I will." Winky grabbed his mug and headed toward the front door.

"Where are you going?"

"I'm rockin' it. Like you said. Shouldn't take but an hour or three to get Maggie back in ship shape. You'll probably take a tad longer."

"Thanks."

Winky grinned. "It'll be all right, Val. You'll see. Keep the coffee coming, will ya?"

"Sure."

"Good. Now, let me get to work."

I limped to the bathroom and shook a blue pain pill out of the bottle. I downed it with a slurp of coffee. I was in my bedroom, contemplating the necessity of wearing a bra when my cellphone buzzed.

"Val, it's Milly."

"Hey."

"Any word about Cold Cuts?"

"Nothing good," I said, and flopped onto the edge of the bed.

"Oh. How are you holding up?"

"Ankle's a lot better. My brain is another story."

"Winky told me you broke up with Tom."

That rat fink. "Wow. Good news travels fast."

"A *joke?* Really?"

"What else am I supposed to do?"

"Listen, Val. Winky's worried about you. So am I. This is serious."

"I know!" My head was thumping and I felt like crying. "But what can I do? Tom wants a decision, and I'm not ready."

"Val, I can't just sit by and watch you blow it and end up living half a life."

"Half a life?"

"You're afraid, Val. I get that."

I bit my lip. "I am *not.*"

"Sure you are. You just don't realize it. Fear doesn't always look like some kind of scary monster, you know. Sometimes it creeps up on you and, I dunno, blocks your ability to see what's right in front of you."

"I don't know what you're talking about."

"Fear makes you wishy-washy. It makes you hang in limbo saying stuff like, 'I don't care.' Or, 'I'll give it a little longer.' I know you Val. You think you're being practical. You think it's safer to keep things the way they are between you and Tom. Call it what you want. It's your choice. But that's *fear*. And that's how you end up living a half a life."

Milly's words cut me to the quick like a lancing knife. I burst into tears. "Milly, what's wrong with me? Why can't I choose? Why is it so...*hard?*"

"Because you keep questioning yourself, Val. You're waiting for something to happen that'll remove all your doubts. But I'm telling you now, it'll never happen. Because it's *you* who's not sure, Val. The certainty you're looking for has to come from inside *you*."

"Is it so wrong to want to be sure?"

"Of course not. I'm not saying you can't question your own heart. I'm just saying you can't question *everybody else's*."

"What if I told you I think Tom's and my relationship is cursed?"

"I'd say you're full of it. You're stalling. You're playing the victim."

"What? I'm not a victim!"

"You're making the choice not to choose, Val. You figure if you never really commit to Tom, it's not your fault if it doesn't work out. You can blame Tom, bad luck, or this stupid curse you're talking about. They're just *excuses*, Val. You're not taking responsibility for your life. You're playing the *poor, pathetic person* that things just happen to. You're playing the *victim*."

"Crap. Maybe you're right, Milly. But I don't want to be taken for granted again. I don't want to disappear –"

"Blah blah blah, Val!" Milly yelled into the phone. "No more excuses. I don't want to hear them. Call me when you grow up!" she snapped, and hung up on me.

My whole body went slack and I fell back onto the bed. Thoughts of Tom swirled in my mind – from how he'd helped me find my real mother to the way his sea-green eyes sparkled whenever he smiled at me. *What more could the man do to convince me? He deserved someone who believed in him without question. Someone who wasn't plagued with doubts. Someone better than me.*

Tears spilled from my eyes until they ran into my ears. I crawled under the covers, my body convulsing from the sobs overtaking me. I buried my throbbing head in the pillow and let the tears flow.

Chapter Thirty-One

M y heart ached as much as my head as I stood in the hot shower and tried to wash away my sorrows. I'd never been very good at knowing what I wanted. I'd been better at knowing what I *didn't* want. I couldn't say I *didn't* want Tom. Was that really good enough?

I dried myself off, got dressed and poured a fresh cup of coffee for Winky. The clock in the kitchen wall said 8:38 a.m. I had taken me three hours to stop crying and clean myself up. I took a deep breath, steeled my resolve, and stepped out the front door.

"Well *there* you are," Winky said, taking the coffee. "You look like my ma after watchin' *Touched by an Angel* on the boob tube."

I sniffed and laughed a short, choking laugh that almost got me crying again. "What's the prognosis on Maggie? Will she make it?"

"I was just about to give her a spin." Winky unhooked the metal rod holding Maggie's heavy hood open. He eased the hood down a few feet, then let gravity finish the job. It clicked shut with the solid, satisfying clunk of sheet metal.

"Great. I could use some fresh air."

"Then climb aboard, Princess Crybaby."

I tried to sneer, but my heart wasn't in it. "Let me grab my purse and we'll be on our way."

"I got the keys already," Winky said.

"I just want to get my phone and license, okay?"

"Might as well take my coffee cup, too. Done drained it dry. Have to say, your coffee's better than Winnie's. But don't you dare tell her I said so."

I smiled, grabbed the cup and went inside. I heard Winky start the engine. I gathered up my purse, then limped over and stuck the key in the front door. I stepped out and turned the lock, then a thought made me open the door again. I looked over at the couch still strewn with legal papers and pizza remains. Winky honked the horn. I scrabbled through the debris on the coffee table until I found what I was looking for. I slipped it into my purse, and limped out the door.

"What took you so long?" Winky asked.

"I forgot something," I said, and slid into the passenger seat. "How about a quick stop at Davie's? I'm starving. How about you?"

"I could always use a donut," Winky said, and rubbed his beer belly.

"And a little sugar from your sweetheart?"

"That never hurt nothin' either," Winky said, and backed Maggie down the driveway.

"I *do* like me a burrito, now and then," Winky said, then swatted down his shirt, which was blown up like a balloon.

We were cruising south on I-275 with the top down. Thanks to Winky's mechanical skills, Maggie had stopped belching smoke and was running like a slightly off-balance top, which was her normal. After a glazed donut and a smooch from Winnie, I'd lured my redneck friend to Sarasota with the promise of a Mahi burrito from Doug's Dugout.

"The guy at the resort told me they're the best," I said.

"That's fine and all," Winky said, "but you ain't foolin' me. I know you want to go snoopin' around that resort. What do you think you'll find out there?"

"Okay, you're right," I confessed. "Like I told you before, whatever happened to Cold Cuts happened on Monday morning. *Somebody* had to see *something*."

"Maybe," Winky said, unconvinced.

"And the desk clerk, Monty? I have a feeling he knows more than he's letting on. A gut feeling, you know?"

"Sure. I know exactly what you're talkin' about," Winky said, his voice more confident. "One time, when I was a kid, my brother told me they was alien bein's from Mars lookin' at us through the winders at night. I thought he was full of crap. Then one night, he showed me a pair of glowin' eyes starin' at us. Well, I flew out the door and run up to the winder. Just like I thought. It what'n no alien from *Mars*."

"What was it?"

"An alien from *Pluto*," Winky said matter-of-factly.

I decided to let that sleeping dog lie.

"YOU SURE ABOUT THIS? What would Tom say?" Winky asked as we pulled into the parking lot at the Sunset Sail-Away Beach Resort.

"It doesn't matter what he'd say," I snarled. Tom was a sore subject, and Winky'd gone and poked it. "Besides, he's gone back to work."

"But what if –"

I cut him off and changed the topic. "Hey, isn't Jorge supposed to find out about his tests today?"

"Yep. That's why I'm stayin' clear of the place. He come back from that retreat actin' like some kinda weirdo. He's always been shy, but now he's just...*creepy* and shy."

"What do you mean?"

"He's all calm-like. Like he ain't got a care in the world. And he's always smilin' like a dog that done ate the Christmas goose."

"Is that so bad?"

"It ain't that it's *bad*, Val. It just ain't *normal*. Not for Jorge. We all got our own kinda normal. It ain't like you notice it much, 'til somebody does something that don't fit. You know what I mean?"

"Yeah. I think I do." I said, and opened the passenger door. "On that note, let's go see if we can find somebody acting abnormal."

"You mean besides you?" Winky joked, and waggled his ginger eyebrows.

"Ha ha," I said, and climbed out of the car.

"ANOTHER STAKEOUT," Winky said, and rubbed his hands together with glee. We were snooping along the tropical path between the resort's lobby and the beach cabana bar.

"For the third time, it's not a *stakeout*," I said. "It's just...a *reconnaissance mission*. Look. See that sign? Number 22. That's the cottage we stayed in."

Winky peered between the crotons and hibiscus bushes. "Looks like they still got the crime scene tape up," he said.

"Crap. I guess that's out. Let's try the lobby."

"What exactly are you looking for, Ms. Fremden?" a stiff voice behind me sounded. I whirled around.

"Uh...I...uh...."

"Well hey there, Tommy Boy," Winky said. "I thought you was at work."

Chapter Thirty-Two

Tom's sea-green eyes seemed dull and elusive as they stared me down. I noticed he glanced at my naked ring finger. "You just can't keep out of trouble, can you?"

"I'm not trying to cause trouble," I snapped, suddenly defensive. "I'm trying to find out what happened to Cold Cuts. And you have no jurisdiction over me, Tom Foreman. I can do what I want."

"Now hey there, you two," Winky said, stepping between us like a referee at a prize fight. He held up his arms. "Hold your horses. Tom, we come down here like Val said. To help find poor old Cold Cuts. She's one of us. We got to do what we can."

Tom's face softened a tiny bit. He looked at Winky. "So, what's your plan?"

Winky nodded toward me. "Ask her. She's the boss."

I smiled condescendingly at Tom, then laid out my masterful plan. "We were just going to wing it," I said.

"Brilliant," Tom deadpanned. "Why didn't *I* think of that?"

Prideful anger made me get creative. "What I *meant*, was, I was going to talk to Monty, the desk clerk. Ask him for my stuff back, and see if I can tell if he's acting...uh...*abnormal*."

"That's right!" Winky said. For a second I thought had come to my rescue. But then he winked hard with his mouth open, like it was all a big joke. "Abnormal!"

"Uh huh," Tom grunted.

"What's *your* brilliant plan?" I sneered at Tom.

He bit his lip. "Not much better," he admitted with a sigh.

My brow furrowed. "Maybe we could work together...."

"Why Monty?" Tom asked, catching me off guard.

"Huh? Well...he kind of runs the place," I said. "And he's the only one I can think of to question besides the old guy in the beekeeper's hat. And nobody's seen him around since the...well...you know."

"Good point," Tom said, as if it cost him to utter the words. "What have we got to lose?"

BRAD PITT'S YOUNG PORTER double didn't appear to know me when I walked into the resort's Hawaiian-inspired lobby. I remembered him, but this time his diamond smile didn't fool me. It was pure cubic zirconia.

"Hello, miss," Brad beamed. "Are you checking in?"

"No. I'd like to talk to the reception clerk," I said. "I believe his name is Monty?"

Brad's smile never wavered. "I'm afraid he's not available."

"Oh. When will he be in?"

"That's very hard to say, miss."

"Who's running the desk, then?"

"I am," Brad said. The phone on the desk began to ring. Brad's smile faltered. He sprinted to the big, black, complicated-looking phone system and hesitated over it, biting his lip.

"Aren't you going to answer that?" I asked.

"Wrong number," Brad said. "Now, perhaps you should come back tomorrow?"

"Perhaps," I said. *Dang it!* With no other strategy, I headed back out the door to the parking lot. Tom was waiting outside.

"Well?" Tom asked.

"Total bust. Where's Winky?"

"Men's room."

Tom and I stood in awkward silence, waiting for Winky to come out.

"Well, at least *you* got to do your business," I said when he finally stumbled out the door.

"No I didn't," Winky said, "on account of some snooty guy wouldn't come out of the only stall in there. What I need to do don't go down a urinal."

"More info than I wanted to know," I said.

"I guess that's it," Tom said, and took a step toward the parking lot.

"Wait a minute," I said to Winky. "What do you mean, *snooty?*"

"Huh? Oh. I dunno. The feller in the stall talked all fancy-like in some weird accent. When I asked how long he planned on sittin' on the john, he said, 'Until you leave, my good sir.' All high and might-like. Now that's what my granny would call one *snooty* fella."

"Oh my word. That sounds like Monty!" I said. "He's holed up in the bathroom because he doesn't want to talk to me. I *knew* something was going on! That Brad kid. He had no idea how to answer the phone...."

"I wouldn't doubt that," Winky agreed. "Poor little fella's been hit with the idiot stick. I seen him talkin' to the door behind that fancy desk. He called it 'Freddie,' and then told it to stay put. Like a door could move. Geeze Louise."

"*Freddie?*" Tom asked. "As in, 'I think Freddie's done it again'?"

I clenched my jaw. "I've got an idea."

"Mahi burritos?" Winky asked.

"No! I want you to go back in the bathroom, Winky, and 'flush out' that snooty guy, so to speak."

Winky grinned. "I think I can handle that."

"Tom, you follow my lead. Pretend to be my attorney."

Tom scowled. "But I made the reservation. Won't he know I'm your...I *was* your...?"

"No chance of that," I said. "They think I'm a lesbian."

"What?" Tom gulped.

I closed my eyes and shook my head. "Don't ask."

"Val, maybe this isn't such a good idea," Tom said. "You have a way of...making things...go...*haywire*."

"And your point is?" I snapped.

"Nothing," Tom sighed.

"Okay then. Let's roll."

"BACK SO SOON, MISS?" Brad's voice cracked as I strolled into the lobby, Tom and Winky at my side. I saw a flash of blue suit disappear into the men's room. Winky nodded at me and took off behind it.

"I really need to speak with Monty," I said. "Why don't you go get him?"

Brad's blue eyes registered panic. "Like I said, he's not here right now."

"Okay then. We'll wait."

We didn't have to wait long. A moment later, Monty came stumbling out of the bathroom, one hand pinching his nose, the other waving away imaginary flies.

"Why Monty, nice to see you again," I said with all the fake sincerity I could muster.

Monty gasped, then stared at me as he marched to his post behind the desk. He appeared shaken, but determined to keep his act together.

"Monty," I began, "do you know anything about Cold Cuts you're not telling me?"

"Of course not, madam," he said. He breathed low and steady to calm himself.

"I just don't see why you're lying," I said. "Unless you had something to do with her disappearance."

"I *didn't*," he barked. "And I don't appreciate your insinuations. Leave now or I'll call the police."

"That won't be necessary," Tom said, and pulled his wallet from the back pocket of his jeans. "I *am* one."

Monty's face turned yellowish green. "I see. But officer...?"

"Foreman," Tom offered.

Monty's eyes lost their focus for a moment, as if preoccupied scanning his memory banks. His eyes bulged when he hit pay dirt. "*Foreman*, you say?" he coughed.

"Yes."

"Well, as I've said before, I know nothing more than –"

"Who's Freddie?" I asked.

Monty choked on his words and hacked up half a lung. "Freddie?"

"Yes. The guy you have locked up in that room behind you," Tom said.

Monty wobbled, as if he might faint. Winky's voice sounded behind us. "Oh, so *that's* what's goin' on. I knew they was *somethin'* fishy about him."

"I...uh...," Monty muttered.

"You going to open that door, or should I call for a warrant?" Tom asked.

Monty's shoulders slumped. "That won't be necessary. Freddie is my uncle. He...um...*owns* this place."

"Why are you holding him in there against his will?" I demanded.

"I'm not holding him against his will. He's not a prisoner. Not like you think," Monty said.

"Then let us see him," Tom demanded.

"He's sleeping. He's an old man," Monty pleaded.

"Last chance," Tom said.

Monty closed his eyes, sighed, and unlocked the door. He opened his eyes again and looked us over. Then he stepped aside and flung the door wide open.

Standing at attention in the doorframe was a naked old man. His head turned in my direction. From underneath his beekeeper's hat he uttered the words, "Hard bodied grubs."

Chapter Thirty-Three

"Well I'll be a Monty's uncle," Winky said, and whistled low and long.

Monty's face drained to alabaster. He collapsed onto a stool behind the reception desk like a punctured balloon.

Old Freddie raised a hand and lifted the shroud on his beekeeper's hat. He whispered to Monty, "Have the Tartan's been vanquished?"

"Yes, Sir Freddie," Monty said tiredly, and rose from his chair. "I'll send a telegraph. Now lay low until the troops arrive."

The old man nodded and laid down on a cot. Monty closed the door, then shook his head and muttered, "I don't get paid enough to put up with this crap anymore."

"What in the world is going on?" Winky asked.

"I can explain," Monty said. "As you can see, my uncle has dementia. We can either keep him here or lock him up in a nursing home. He used to live in cottage 22, but now he needs too much supervision. That's why I keep him in there. It's not a prison, I assure you."

A knock sounded from the other side of the door. "Excuse me," Monty said, and opened the door a crack.

"Bring me the Tiddly Winks, you heathen!" the old man whispered.

"Yes, very good, sir." Monty closed the door and faced us again, his haughty façade totally erased.

"I used to like playin' me some Tiddly Winks," Winky offered.

"Cottage 22," I said. "That's the one *I* was in. Do you think your uncle might have...I dunno, gone there and thought Cold Cuts was an intruder? I left the door unlocked. Could he have –"

"My uncle's harmless, I swear," Monty said. "He spends his time fishing and...in there." He nodded toward the door.

"Why did it take so long to get my room ready that day?" I asked. "The police reports said it was cleaned up. But they used...uh...Luminet?" I looked at Tom.

"Luminol," Tom offered. "The SCI report showed that the room had recently been spattered in blood and cleaned up."

Monty sighed. "Like I said. That's Freddie's old cottage. Sometimes he forgets – or remembers – hard to tell. Anyway, sometimes he goes back there and tries to get in. Your room wasn't ready on Sunday because Freddie had caught a huge tarpon and filleted it in there. It took them forever to get the blood stains out of the carpet and bedspreads."

"Who is 'them'?" Tom asked.

"I hired a professional cleanup company," Monty said.

"Which one?" Tom asked.

"Vellum Vistas," Monty said.

"They're crime-scene cleaners. You just happened to have their number handy?" Tom asked.

"No. Well, yes. My uncle is a pretty...*active* fisherman."

"Could they have overlooked some of the blood or fish parts?"

"No."

"Then how do you explain this?" I said, and held up the tarpon scale I'd lifted from my coffee table. "It was in my hair when I got home."

"I'm the one found that!" Winky beamed.

"I don't know," Monty said. "I guess anything is possible."

"A pair of bloody pliers and a tooth were also recovered the day *after* your professional cleanup," Tom said, "along with a blood trail from the cottage to the beach. If your uncle could carry a huge fish like a tarpon and butcher it, then it's highly likely he's capable of, in a delusional state, doing the same thing to a human...." Tom's voice trailed off.

"I just can't see him doing that," Monty said. "But I'll come clean with you. He picked the lock Sunday night. He was unaccounted for...for a few hours."

"How many hours?" I asked.

"All night," Monty confessed.

"Do you think he's capable of pulling out someone's tooth?" Tom asked.

"Yes," Monty sighed. "He's done it before."

"What?" I almost screeched.

Monty sighed. "He was a dentist before he became an hotelier."

"Hotelier," giggled Winky. "That sounds funny."

I gave Winky the evil eye.

"What's the full name of your uncle?" Tom asked.

"William F. Rockbottom," Monty said.

"I ran the plates of every car in your lot," Tom said. "That was one of the names."

"Yes. That's him."

"He still *drives?*" I asked, incredulous.

"No. Not technically."

"What does that mean?" Tom asked.

"We have to keep the keys locked up," Monty explained. "If Freddie finds a set, he'll...you know, try to take off."

"So your uncle can carry and butcher a huge, 60-90 pound fish, he can drive, and he was missing during the time Cold Cuts disappeared," Tom said. "What's your financial position in this resort, Monty?"

"Excuse me?" Monty said, startled by the question.

"You got any clams in the place." Winky explained.

"I...uh...don't see how that's relevant."

"Well then, let me make it clearer," Tom said. "Suppose you're in line to inherit this place. If your Uncle Freddie went and murdered someone, you might lose everything you've been so diligently working for."

"Confound it!" Monty snapped. "I never thought of that. He tricked me, that little turd."

"Who did?" I asked.

"Freddie's idiot son. Monday morning, he made me help him load a piece of rolled up carpet into an old RV on the lot. I saw blood dripping out of it. He told me to keep quiet about it. He said it was in everybody's interest that I keep my mouth shut. He didn't tell me anything else, so I couldn't rat him out, I assume."

"And Freddie's son is...?"

"William F. Rockbottom, IV," Monty said. "But he goes by the stupid name of Bill Robo."

Chapter Thirty-Four

"**B**ill Robo? Where is he now?" I bellowed at Monty. He shrunk back as if I'd struck him in the face with a dirty flyswatter.

"I don't know," Monty said. "I haven't heard a word from him since I helped him load the body in the RV. I *swear*."

"Did *Bill* do it, or was he covering for your uncle?" Tom asked through clenched jaws.

Monty's face went slack for a moment, as if he was pondering the question for the first time. He shook his head softly. "I honestly couldn't tell you for certain. I'm sorry."

"Who says Bill ain't coverin' for *your* snooty butt?" Winky asked.

We all stared at Monty. His eyes grew wide and he stuck his nose in the air. "I'm *British*, not American. We don't solve disputes by killing each other."

"Why does your cousin Bill use an alias?" Tom asked. "Does he have a criminal record?"

Monty sighed. "He got in a spot of trouble a while back. When he was a teenager. He's always been a little...*different*. That's why Freddie asked me to come over and help out. His son is...*unreliable*, to put it mildly."

"You said he got in trouble." I said. "What did he do?"

"He was charged with car theft, reckless driving and...," Monty sighed again, "kidnapping."

"Geeze!" I said.

"I don't get it," Winky said. "If he didn't have no wreck, why was he charged with wreck-less driving?"

Tom and I turned and shouted at the same time. "Winky!"

Winky took a step backward. "'Scuze me! Just trying to get the facts straight."

"So Bill's done this before," I said to Monty.

"If he kidnapped your friend, and took her vehicle, then, yes. But if he uh...*killed* her...I couldn't tell you for sure if it was his first...you know...*murder*."

"Any idea where he might have gone with the RV?" Tom asked.

"None."

"Do you know if he had a friend...a woman with red hair?" I asked.

"Bill's a trust-fund beach bum. He always has 'friends' around. I gave up trying to keep track of them all a long time ago."

Brad came through the lobby door with a couple of new guests. The way Monty looked at the young porter, it was probably Brad's last chance for a good tip.

"I have to keep things going here," Monty said to us. "The place would fall down around my ears if I didn't work twenty-four seven. I don't have the time or energy to kill someone...much less plot their disposal. I don't mean to be rude, but I really need to check these folks in."

"Okay," Tom said. "We'll be in touch if we need anything else. Thanks for your cooperation."

"You're in America now," Winky said to Monty. "You need to learn you how to speak good, proper English, feller."

Monty blew out a breath that contained the last of his patience, then turned and plastered on a fake smile for the tourists. I almost felt sorry for him.

"Come on, Winky," I said, and tugged on his arm. "We're done here."

We left the lobby and headed to our cars.

"I guess that's all we can do for now," Tom said. "I'll stop by the Sarasota station and fill in Detective Stanley. It should be enough for him to put out an APB for the RV."

"I hope it doesn't land you in any trouble, Tom," I said. "Thanks for your help."

"Sure," he said solemnly. "But you don't need my help, Val. You handled yourself pretty well in there." He looked down at my hand. His eyes lingered on the place where his ring used to be. "It looks like you're doing all right on your own."

"So what happens next?" Winky blurted.

"Well, I guess that depends on the boss." Tom said. He shot me a glance, then turned and walked away.

"WELL, AT LEAST YOU didn't hit Rockbottom," Winky joked as I pulled out of the resort's parking lot. He'd meant to make me laugh, but his words cut through me like a hot knife through Crisco. They'd hit way too close to home.

I poked my chin up and turned the radio on full blast to drown out Winky's voice and the thoughts percolating like rancid coffee inside my head. When I'd finally dropped him off at Davie's Donuts, I'd gone home, put on my pajamas and crawled into bed.

I was physically and emotionally spent. As I sunk down in the pillows, the doorbell rang.

"Who the hell could be bothering me at this hour?" I muttered. I looked at the clock. It was 6:33 p.m.

Laverne was at the door. "Did you hear the news?" she asked, wriggling with excitement like a wormy puppy.

"No."

"Jorge passed his tests! Isn't that fantastic!"

I mustered all the enthusiasm I could, considering the facts that Cold Cuts was probably dead, and so was my relationship with Tom. "That's great."

"They're having a little party at Caddy's to celebrate tomorrow." Laverne's grin straightened out a notch. "Hey. What's gotten into you?" She grabbed my hand. "You're not wearing that horrible ring, are you?" She examined my fingers to make sure it wasn't on one of them.

"No," I said, and yanked my hand away. There was no use telling Laverne the bad news about Cold Cuts until it was official. So I told her about Tom and me, instead. "Tom and I aren't doing so well."

"Because of the ring?"

I hadn't really put the two together until she'd said that.

"Laverne, Tom found that ring and gave it to *me*. Do you think that means that *he's*...that *we're* bad luck together? I mean, what are the odds that a girl who was found on the side of the road would be given an engagement ring that her boyfriend found on the side of the road?"

Laverne cocked her horsey head. "I don't think Tom's to blame, Val. It's the ring. And *you*."

"What do you mean, *me?*" I said, on the defensive. "*You're* the one who brought this ring into our lives in the first place."

Laverne winced. "That's true, and I'm sorry, honey. I don't know if it's too late to save Cold Cuts or not. But Val, it's not too late to save yourself."

"From the curse of Vendaygo?"

"From the curse of *yourself*."

"What are you talking about?"

"Honey, you're so afraid of making a mistake you don't know a good thing when it's staring you in the face."

I blew out a heavy sigh. "Not *this* again."

"Yes, *this* again," Laverne snapped. "Because you *still* haven't got it. I used to be like you, Val. I had a list of what my prince charming had to be to meet my criteria. Rich. Good looking. Generous. Loyal. And a firm backside."

Laverne swatted her own bottom for emphasis.

"So?" I muttered.

"One day I realized, if I ever met the guy who had everything I wanted, I'd be scared wit-less of him. He'd be too good for me!"

I pursed my doubting lips. "Is there a point to all this?"

"Take my advice, honey. A laundry list of stuff won't make love work. In the end, all love comes down to is whether you can stand the way a man chews his cornflakes in the morning."

I burst into tears. "I'm too picky, Laverne! I'll never be happy!"

"Oh, honey! Now don't give up on being happy. I'm just saying give up on *perfection*. Including your own." She wiped a tear from my face. "Trust me. It'll never happen."

I sniffed. "Laverne, do you think if you had loved Vinnie, the ring wouldn't have been cursed?"

Laverne cocked her head to think. "Maybe. But you *love* Tom, and look what happened when you wore it."

"That's true." I flopped on the couch. "Wait. Oh my lord, Laverne!"

"What?" Laverne ran over and sat beside me. "Are you okay, honey?"

"I just realized something. All those bad things that happened. They happened when I *wasn't* wearing the ring."

Laverne cocked her horsey head. "Huh?"

"Think about it. I wasn't wearing the ring at the resort when Cold Cuts disappeared. It was in the garbage disposal, remember?"

Laverne's hand flew to her mouth. "My word! That's right!"

"I wasn't wearing it when the tornado hit. Or when I got kicked in the head with a manikin leg. Or when I was attacked by crickets."

"Crickets?" Laverne asked.

"And when Tom and I had our fight and broke up...*I wasn't wearing the ring.*"

"Honey, maybe that ring has the *opposite effect* on you," Laverne said. "Maybe it takes away your bad luck when you wear it, because...." Laverne caught herself and stopped mid-sentence.

"Because my usual luck is for crap, right?"

Laverne shrugged and smiled sheepishly.

"You may have a point, there, Laverne. Thank you." I leaned over and searched through the debris on the coffee table until I found the ring. I slipped it on my finger. "I think I'll test my luck," I said.

Laverne smiled and hugged me. "Then I'll leave you to it, honey. I'm rooting for you."

I watched Laverne and her gold high heels go out the door, then through the yard back toward her house. I shut the door behind her, then picked up my cellphone and swallowed hard. I hit speed dial #7, for Tom, and listened as it ring. He didn't pick up. His strong, kind voice on the recording, invited me to leave a message after the beep.

I squeezed my words out around the huge lump in my throat. "Tom? If it's not too late...I want you, too."

Chapter Thirty-Five

It was hard to believe only five days had passed since life as I'd known it had been blown apart. I'd waited by the phone, but Tom didn't call that night. At midnight, I'd given up and drowned my rejection in a bottle of red wine and the remains of a leftover pizza. Then I'd limped to bed for the first time in years without brushing my teeth or washing my face.

I woke up the next morning with breath so bad I disgusted myself. I checked for a phone message from Tom. Nothing. I was putting the phone back on the nightstand when it rang in my hand.

"Hello?"

"Good morning, honey!" Laverne's cheerful voice reverberated in my hungover head like a ricocheted bullet.

"Hi," I croaked.

"Should I pick you up for the party?"

"What party?"

"Jorge's celebration party. At Caddy's."

"Oh. I don't know...I don't –"

"What's wrong? Didn't you work it out with Tom last night?"

"I called and left a message. He didn't call back."

"Oh."

"He'll be there, Laverne. At the party."

"Sure he will, honey. But you're going to have to face it sometime. Life goes on."

"For some of us, I guess. But I can't go. I'm a total wreck."

"I can help you out with that. I'll be right over."

"But –" Laverne clicked off the phone. I looked at the clock. It was 10:57 a.m. *Geeze. I'd slept half the day away.*

Crap on a cracker! I forgot to call Mr. Charles to let him know the latest!

I dialed the number and waited for the recorder to beep. "Mr. Charles? Bill Robo is actually William F. Rockbottom, IV. He has a history of kidnapping, but his father could have been the one – it's complicated. Call me."

IN MY DEFENSE, I DIDN'T have the will power to resist Laverne's fashion assault. My mind had been clouded with thoughts of Cold Cuts and Tom, and I hadn't realized Laverne had been teasing my hair until it was already the size of a basketball. I patted at my afro while she decked me out in the full Vegas-style makeup treatment.

One look in the bathroom mirror and I gave up on any thought of personal dignity. When Laverne came at me with a red sweater she'd brought from her private collection, I'd thought, *what the hell*. I slipped it on over my jeans. It was the perfect complement. I looked like a clown that had narrowly escaped an explosion at a rhinestone factory.

"You look gorgeous," Laverne said. "You'll knock Tom's socks off in that!"

"Unless he's not wearing any," I said, and smiled weakly. I twisted the ring on my finger. I couldn't decide whether to wear it or not. *Would it tick Tom off if I did? Or would it help break the iceberg between us?*

"Let's get going, honey," Laverne said, and gathered up her pile of makeup tubes and bottles and compacts. "I don't want to be late."

"It's not like we have to be there on the dot," I argued.

"Yes we do," Laverne said. "I made the cake."

My gut gurgled involuntarily. "Well, in that case, let's get this party started."

"Why are they holding it at that old shack Caddy's?" Laverne asked as we went out the front door.

"Well, it's kind of fitting, Laverne. "That's where the guys and I all met. You know, because of Glad."

"Oh," Laverne said, and winked at me. "Well then, that makes it the perfect place for you all to get back together again, too."

WHEN I WALKED ONTO the open air porch at Caddy's with Laverne, the jovial, carefree atmosphere dried up like a piss in the desert. I couldn't tell if everyone was shocked to silence by my appearance or the sight of Laverne's cake.

"She's gone and done done it again," Winky said, his voice hollow and husky as if he'd been punched in the gut.

"I think she looks fine," Winnie said, and elbowed Winky in the ribs.

"Huh?" Winky grunted. "That ain't what I'm talk –"

"Congratulations, Jorge!" I said, and set the cake on a picnic table. "Beautiful day for a party!"

Jorge looked up at the blue sky and grinned. "It sure is."

Music started playing over the bar's stereo. "This really *is* my lucky day, I guess," Jorge said. "'Cause they're playing my favorite song. I feel like dancing!"

"Then let's dance," I said. I set my purse beside the cake, and took Jorge's hand. "I'm so proud of you, Jorge."

"Thanks. You know, you're looking pretty fancy for a little beach party."

I wiggled my butt. "It's shake and quake, and Laverne helped."

"Oh," Jorge laughed. "That explains it."

"Anyway, this isn't just some little beach party. It's a celebration of your new start, Jorge. You've got a whole new life ahead of you!"

Jorge twirled me around. I tripped on my feet and spun right into Tom.

"Ooops! I'm so sorry," I said, before I knew it was him.

"Just watch yourself," he said. He set me back on my feet and marched toward Goober and the rest of the gang.

I tried to resume my dance with Jorge, but I'd lost my rhythm. "Do you mind if we stop?" I asked Jorge. "I'm just not...."

"Jes, I do," Jorge answered. He grabbed my hand and pulled me close, then twirled me around again like a professional tango dancer.

"Wow! You're a pretty good dancer," I said.

"Val, when Winky shot me in the face with that water gun, it made me question my dream of being a policeman again. But I didn't give up. I got through it, and I feel more confident than I have in forever. You and Tom. You'll work it out. You'll get through it, too."

"I dunno, Jorge. Your future's looking bright. Mine's going down the drain."

"It ain't over 'til it's over."

The song ended.

"It's over," I said.

Jorge shrugged and let me go. We joined the group sitting around the picnic table. The sun was shining bright on their faces, but instead of being festive, the atmosphere felt more like a funeral dirge. The dour faces eyeballing Laverne's cake made me a tear escape down my cheek.

"I...I'm sorry," I said. "I don't know why I'm so emotional."

"That time of month?" Winky deadpanned.

"Or maybe it's 'the change,' Goober said. "You know, fifty is the new f-word, after all."

"You boys stop teasing Val," Laverne said. She turned to me, "There's nothing wrong with you honey. You're just like a lot of women out there. The only thing you've lost is your confidence."

My face felt as if it had caught fire. I wanted to disappear. I grabbed my purse, then realized I'd ridden over with Laverne. I couldn't escape, so I ran to the ladies room. One look in the mirror and I was almost too embarrassed to call a cab. My phone rang. I didn't recognize the number.

"Hello?"

What I heard next made me forget my insignificant little problems. I marched out of the ladies room. Tom was coming out of the men's room at the exact same moment.

"Tom!" I said. "I need –"

His sea-green eyes brewed like a storm. "What do you want me to do for you this time, *if it's not too late?*"

I swallowed my pride. It wasn't as hard as I thought it would be. "Just one more thing, please. I need you to go with me to the morgue. My friend Darren called. He said Cold Cuts' body just turned up there."

"Aww crap, Val," Tom said. He looked over at the group. "There's no point in spoiling Jorge's party right now. Follow me to my car."

Chapter Thirty-Six

It was the longest fifteen-minute ride of my life. Inside the SUV, the space between Tom and me was crammed to capacity with unsaid words and melancholy memories. Why was it so hard to put our differences aside? I was wasting my life. But Cold Cuts no longer had a life to waste.

When we pulled into the parking lot of the county morgue, I nearly screamed. Parked by the front entrance was Glad's old RV.

"What's going on? Did that butcher bring her back?" I asked.

"Nothing would surprise me anymore," Tom spat.

A man got out of the RV and walked toward the front door of the building.

"That's him!" I screeched. "That's Bill Robo!"

Tom nearly kicked his door open. He ran like a quarterback up to the man and tackled him from behind. Tom had Robo pinned on the asphalt and his hands in cuffs before I could limp over to them.

"How could you do it, you monster?" I hissed at Robo.

"Do what?" Robo asked, his voice strained under the pressure of Tom's knee in his back.

"Hey! Lay off him!" I heard a voice say behind me. I turned to see a red-headed woman with a face just like Cold Cuts'.

I was just about to punch her in the nose when I realized it *was* Cold Cuts. "What the hell!"

"I could say the same thing," she said. "What are you doing to Bill?"

"What are *you* doing *alive?*" I screeched. "We thought he murdered you!"

"What? Who?"

"*You* disappeared. *He* disappeared. There was blood...." I gave up trying to explain and grabbed hold of my friend, "You're alive!" I squeezed Cold Cuts tight.

"Of course I'm alive....what's –"

Suddenly, the doors to the morgue burst open. Darren Dudley came running out. "Ha ha! Got you! Good, Valliant Stranger!" he yelled.

If I'd had hold of Tom's gun, I'd have shot him dead.

IT SEEMED STRANGE TO be at Davie's Donuts without Winnie and Winky. But it was even stranger to hear the tale Cold Cuts and Bill had to tell.

"I woke up late and decided to dye my hair," Cold Cuts said, and took a nibble from a powdered donut. "I went out to the RV to get the dye, and ran into that crazy old fisherman guy. You know, the one with –"

"The beekeeper's hat," I said impatiently. "Yes, go on."

"He followed me back to the cottage. It creeped me out, so I told Bill about it. He said he'd take care of it and went outside."

"Wait. Back up. When did you meet Bill that morning?" Tom asked. He was sitting beside me in the booth. Cold Cuts and Bill sat opposite us, snuggling like love birds while Tom and I kept a cool distance from each other.

"Uh...he spent the night with me...with *us* in the cottage," Cold Cuts explained.

"Oh," I said.

"Don't tell me you didn't notice, Val. He snores like a little piglet!" Cold Cuts nudged Bill on the shoulder. The portions of his cheeks not covered with beard blushed as he coughed out a laugh.

"No, I didn't know," I said. "I thought maybe it had been that crazy fisher – I mean, your father, Bill."

Bill laughed. "He *is* crazy. And he's a fisherman, all right. While Cold Cuts dyed her hair, I went out to check on Pops. I found him trying to break into the cottage window. He'd dragged a bloody tarpon up from the beach and wanted to fillet it in there. I tried to convince him otherwise, but as you know, he's a big guy. And when he sets his squirrely mind to something...."

"Anyway," Cold Cuts said, "Bill came barging in the bathroom just as I was rinsing the color out of my hair in the sink. I couldn't see. I thought it was the lunatic – Bill's dad. I jerked my head back, and dye went everywhere!"

"It was actually me," Bill said. "I'd been trying to keep Pops outside while I ran in and told Cold Cuts I needed to take care of him. But when she made that mess in the bathroom, I thought, what was the point, now? I let Pops come in and lay in Cold Cuts' bed. I told him it was the best place to hide from the paratroopers. Anyway, I explained the whole crazy situation to Cold Cuts. And Pops was a good boy. He stayed under the covers while we sorted out what to do with him, the fish and the whole bloody mess."

"It was my idea to load the tarpon into the RV," Cold Cuts said. "I told Bill we could get rid of it on the way to the keys."

"What?"

"Oh. I forgot that part. Bill and I decided to go camping in the RV."

"Without even telling me?" I snapped.

"What? No. I left you a note."

"I didn't get it. Wait. It must have been blown away in the tornado...."

"What tornado?" Bill and Cold Cuts asked in unison.

"Not important at the moment," Tom said. "Continue."

Bill nodded. "I went and grabbed a carpet out of my place and wrapped the tarpon in it, but it was too heavy for me to move by myself. So I went and got Monty to help me. When we got done with that, Monty and I tried to get Pops out of bed, but he put up a scuffle. By the time we wrangled him up, I noticed he had a bit of a bloody lip, and a cut on his hand. Anyway, we got Pops back into his...the place by the reception desk...and I took off with Cold Cuts. Monty was supposed to send someone to clean up the room."

"I guess the tornado interrupted his plans," I said. "But what about the bloody pliers under the mattress? And the tooth?"

"You're kidding," Bill said, and shook his head. "He was a dentist, you know. If he gets a loose tooth, he yanks it out himself. Wait...that might explain his bloody mouth."

"And the cut on his hand could explain the blood trail from the beach," Tom said.

"But it doesn't explain why you didn't call," I whined at Cold Cuts.

"I *did*. In the note, I told you we were headed to Key West. I said I'd text you when we arrived. I sent you a funny text. Didn't you get it?"

"I got a text with a picture of you with your throat slashed. From Halloween."

"Oh. That's weird. I meant to send you a pic of us on the beach." Cold Cuts shrugged. "Oops. My bad."

"I was worried sick!" I snapped. "I tried to call you back. You didn't answer."

"I'd used up my battery. And I forgot my phone charger. I didn't have enough juice to even check messages until today. We stopped at a coffee shop and I was able to get a partial charge. I sent you a text saying we were back, but you didn't respond."

I checked my phone. Sure enough. There was a text from Cold Cuts. "I missed it."

"Anyway, I got a text from this guy Darren saying he was a friend of yours. He told me we should all meet at his place. He gave me the address. I didn't realize it was the city morgue until we pulled in. He came out and told us you liked pranks, and that he needed our help to pull one off on you. I told him you weren't that keen. But I went inside anyway, to use the restroom. When I came back out, I found Tom crouched on top of Bill like he was some kind of criminal."

"Are you a criminal?" I asked Bill.

"No," he said.

"Then why the alias?" Tom asked.

Bill sighed. "My name is William F. Rockbottom, IV. What would you do with a name like that? I just...shortened it. You know. Bill for William. Robo for Rock-Bottom. That's not a crime."

"Monty told us you've been charged with kidnapping and car theft before," I said.

Bill blew out a big breath. "Monty *would* be that dramatic. Listen, when I was seventeen, my girlfriend at the time wanted to go see a movie. Her father said no. I had my license, but no car. I thought I'd be a hero in her eyes. I 'borrowed' her father's station wagon and drove us to the theater. When we walked out, the police were waiting. I got charged with kidnapping and car theft and reckless driving, even though nobody had even seen us leave. What can I say? Her father didn't want me seeing her, so he took care of me. He was a real douche."

"Geeze, did we get this wrong," I said. "We thought you'd kidnapped Cold Cuts and stole the RV. Maybe even...you know...*killed* her."

"Innocent on all charges," Cold Cuts said.

"Sorry about the rough treatment," Tom said to Bill. "No hard feelings, I hope?"

"You were looking out for my girl," Bill said, and kissed Cold Cuts lightly on the lips. "How could I blame you for that?"

"So, that's it," Tom said. "Unbelievable. I'm really glad you're okay, Cold Cuts. Excuse me, but I need to go make some calls now. I really am glad this all worked out. You two make a cute couple."

Tom got up and left.

"I'm sorry if I worried you, Val," Cold Cuts said. "I really had no idea you didn't get my note when I left. And the whole text thing...bummer!"

"It's all right now. I'm just glad you're okay." My phone chirped. It was a text from Finkerman.

"So that clears everything up, I guess?" Cold Cuts said.

"Well, almost everything," I said. I looked at the cozy pair and forced a smiled. "You two by chance in the mood for a party?"

Chapter Thirty-Seven

It took three days for everyone's guts to get back to normal after eating Laverne's cake – less time than it took to set the record straight with the Sarasota Police Department. But even though the charges were dropped, I still had two angry cops to deal with. My situation with Tom was no better. And the fifteen-grand lawsuit with Detective Stanley was still unresolved.

I hadn't talked to Tom since that day at Davie's Donuts. I still didn't know what to say to him. Oddly enough, I'd had better luck with Finkerman. He'd agreed to my request for a mediation session with his client. I'd just arrived at Finkerman's office, where I was to meet with him and Detective Stanley. I'd brought along my own back-up team.

"You brought Penelope Piddleton with you?" Detective Stanley said as we entered the mediation room. The place was as barren, grim and listless as I'd imagined it would be.

"This is not acceptable," Finkerman said. "She's your *accomplice*, for crying out loud."

"Gentlemen, we're not here to pick a fight," I said. "I promise you'll find her presence here...*pertinent*."

"Humph," Finkerman grunted, but acquiesced.

Cold Cuts and I took seats together on the opposite side of a cheap, grey Formica table.

"Well?" Finkerman said impatiently. "What's your proposal?"

"First, Cold Cuts and I want to apologize to Detective Stanley. We never intended for anything like what happened to...you know...*happen*."

"Right," Finkerman said. "But I think my client will be comforted more by the feeling of fifteen grand in his pocket." He turned to Stanley. "Am I right?" Stanley sneered and nodded his agreement.

"Well, as you know, money can't buy everything," I said.

"*Most* everything," Finkerman retorted. "And you can steal the rest."

"It can't buy *looks*, for example," I continued, ignoring Finkerman. "Or sex appeal."

"I beg to differ," Finkerman sneered.

"I mean *real* sex appeal," I said. "Not the kind measured by how thick your wallet is, or how shiny your toys are."

Finkerman's face reddened. He pursed his lips. "What's your point?"

"The point is, we want to offer Detective Stanley not just an apology, but a...a...a –"

"A makeover," Cold Cuts said. "From a *woman's* point of view."

"Wha –" Finkerman objected.

"Hear her out," I said. "She's a professional. She works with movie stars!"

Cold Cuts' back straightened. "Yes. I work in movies and TV. And I believe Detective Stanley has excellent...uh...bone structure. Truly rugged good looks."

"Give me a break," Finkerman laughed. He looked over at Stanley, who didn't seem to share Finkerman's opinion of him.

Stanley puffed up in his chair. "I want to hear what Ms. Piddleton has to say, if you don't mind, Ferrol."

Finkerman clapped his trap shut and glared at us. "Proceed."

Cold Cuts reached to her side, then placed on the table an expensive-looking leather container about the size and shape of a cigar box.

"If Detective Stanley is willing to drop his lawsuit, I am prepared to offer him my prized possession," she said softly.

Finkerman crinkled his nose. "A bunch of cigars? Fifteen grand can buy –"

"No. Not cigars," Cold Cuts said, cutting him off. "A one-of-a-kind, custom hairpiece. Created for and worn by the legendary, super-sexy movie star Logan Greene."

"Logan Greene didn't wear a toupee!" Finkerman sneered.

"Exactly," Cold Cuts said. "No one ever suspected a thing."

I could see the gears turning behind Detective Stanley's horrid toupee. "I want it!" he bellowed, and lurched across the table toward the box. "Give it to me!"

Cold Cuts picked up the box and smiled. "Just sign the papers dropping the case, and I'll show you how to wear it like the king that you are."

I pushed the papers toward Detective Stanley and handed him a pen. He hesitated for a split second and looked over at Finkerman, who was opening and closing his mouth like a fish out of water. Stanley shook his jowly head at him, uncapped the pen and scribbled away.

It was my turn to sneer at Finkerman.

Stanley shoved the signed documents back my way.

"Very good," Cold Cuts said. "Please, Detective Stanley, follow me." She stood and led Stanley into the ladies' room.

Finkerman sighed and slumped back in his seat. "Well played, Ms. Fremden. Well played."

"I PROMISED YOU A MAKEOVER for your birthday, and I delivered," Cold Cuts said as we climbed into Shabby Maggie.

"You sure did. And then some." I turned the ignition and let Maggie's glass-pack mufflers roar. "Tell me. Did that wig really belong to Logan Greene?"

"Does it really matter?" she laughed. "Anything was better than this dead rat." She held up the mangy old squirrel pelt that once disgraced Detective Stanley's greasy pate. "What should I do with it?"

"Yuck! Fling it out the.... Wait! I've got an idea."

We made a pit stop at the post office. I dug an old shoebox out of my trunk. "Who should we say it's from?" I asked.

"Your secret admirer," Cold Cuts suggested.

"Perfect."

We waited in line, then watched the postal clerk wrap the box in brown paper. "Any hazardous materials inside?"

"You could say that," Cold Cuts smirked.

"She's just joking," I said.

The clerk eyed us dubiously and slapped the postage sticker on the box. Cold Cuts and I giggled like idiots as he placed it into the mail drop. Sometime in the coming week, Darren Dudley would have another disgusting dead body to deal with.

"WHAT'S GOING TO HAPPEN with you and Bill?" I asked Cold Cuts as we pulled into my driveway. Her old RV was parked in the street.

"I dunno. I guess we'll play it by ear."

"I wish I could be so happy-go-lucky."

"It's better not to try to force things to fit," Cold Cuts said, and climbed out of the car. "I'd better get going. It's a bit of a drive back to Sarasota, and I want to miss rush hour."

"Okay," I climbed out of the car and followed her to the RV. "I'll see you at Milly's wedding next week, right?"

"Yes. Wouldn't miss it." Cold Cuts hopped in the RV and shut the door, then rolled down the window. "And cheer up about Tom. People come into our lives to play roles we asked them to, Val. They say the worst roles go to the ones who love you the most."

"Geeze. What's that supposed to mean?"

"Actions, Val," Cold Cuts said, and turned the ignition. The old RV sputtered to life. "Actions speak louder than words. Don't think about what you two might have said in a moment of anger. Words are cheap. Think about what you two have done together. How you feel when you're with him. That's what *really* matters."

I nodded and watched the RV head down the road. Then I looked and saw a dwarf coming out Laverne's front door.

I hadn't noticed the white Mercedes in Laverne's drive when I'd pulled up. Mr. Fellows saw me, flinched, and then waved.

"Thanks for the papers!" I called after him. "It worked! I'm off the hook!"

"That's great!" he called back.

Laverne came out of the house, saw me and did a double take. She said something to Mr. Fellows. He waved one more time, got in his Mercedes and left. Laverne headed inside.

I smelled a fish. "Laverne, wait up!"

Laverne stood frozen with her hand on the doorknob.

"What's going on?" I asked. "Are you getting sued or something?"

"Lord, no," Laverne said, obviously relieved.

"Then what's Mr. Fellows doing here?"

"I'm getting, old, honey," Laverne explained. "I gotta think about dying. And what'll happen to my stuff when I do. I didn't want to leave a mess behind...you know, like Tony and Glad did to you."

"Oh. Okay." I turned to head back to my house, but the words Laverne blurted next stopped me in my tracks.

"All right! We're having an affair, okay?"

"What?" I whipped back around. "You and Mr. Fellows?"

"Yes. JD asked me not to say anything. He didn't want to make things weird between us."

"So why are you confessing now? You're usually good at keeping secrets."

"This is one secret I can't keep any longer. I've got to tell someone or I'm gonna bust. Val, *I'm in love!*"

"In *love?* Wow...that's fantastic! How long have you been –"

"We got together when you were at your mom's over Christmas. We didn't have anything else to do. One thing led to another and...we found out we liked each other's company."

So wait...I really *did* see a dwa...I mean *Mr. Fellows* at your place that time I had the flu. When you made me the soup."

"Yes. It could be."

Chapter Thirty-Eight

Everyone was having a happy ending except Tom and me. Another week of angst had come and gone without a word between us. Tom's actions were speaking loud and clear. It was over between us.

I guess Laverne had been right all along. The engagement ring *was* cursed. But when I really thought about it, I just couldn't believe my love life could be determined by a *ring*. After all, when it came to love, I'd generated a load of rotten luck all on my own.

I twisted the ring on my finger. I was still wearing it because I'd been intrigued by something Laverne had said. Namely that, in my case, the ring's curse might be reversed. Because my life was already plagued with bad luck, the ring might somehow have the opposite effect for me. Instead of making bad things happen, the ring might keep me safe from disaster as long as I wore it.

Weirdly, so far, Laverne's theory had borne itself out as true. The last week had passed without incident. My life was calm. Work was fine. Maggie was running okay. And not a single, solitary, crazy thing had happened to me. Everything was back to what most people would call 'normal.' But to me, it felt oddly like *someone else's* normal.

I sighed and smoothed the front of my pale-blue, satin dress. I locked the door behind me and headed to Sunset Beach for Milly and Vance's wedding. As Milly's Maid of Honor, I had two jobs. I was to hold Milly's bouquet during the ceremony, and I was to find a place to ditch the wedding cake Laverne had made for the occasion. The horrid

hunk of icing-covered gastric distress was in the trunk of my car, awaiting its demise. Somewhere across town, Jorge was putting the finishing
touches on its stunt double.

THERE WEREN'T TOO MANY covert places to dump a dead cake
body between my place and Sunset Beach. The only sure bet was a
dumpster hidden behind the sea oats in St. Pete Beach's public beach
parking lot. When I drove up to it, I got more than I bargained for. The
dumpster was nearly full to the brim with smelly picnic leftovers and
busted beach chairs.

And parked two spots away was a silver 4Runner.

"Crap!" I muttered. "This is all I need." I checked my face in the
mirror, and slipped the ring off my finger. If that was Tom, I didn't need
him thinking I was pining away for him.

I climbed out and opened the trunk with the key. Lying inside was
the most hideous wedding cake I'd ever seen. It looked like a melted
snowman that had been pissed on by a horde of winos.

"Sorry, Laverne," I said, and hoisted the thirty-pound monstrosity
out of the trunk. I faltered in my high heels as I sidestepped the over-
flow of smelly garbage, but recovered and inched my way until I was
about a foot from the dumpster. The rim on the thing was higher than
I thought. I realized I'd have to lift the cake over my head to heave it in.

I bent at the knees, grunted, and hoisted the monstrosity over my
head. I wobbled on my heels, arched the cake too far back and lost my
balance. The cake and I went tumbling backward.

But I didn't fall far.

Someone's arms caught me.

"You didn't happen to take any Nyquil, did you?" Tom's voice
sounded behind me.

I cringed and shut my eyes. "No."

"I know you hate weddings, Val. But this is ridiculous."

I turned to find the cake had missed me, but not Tom. His shoulder was covered in gooey white slime punctuated with blackish cake crumbs. "Oh, geeze," I muttered. "I'm sorry."

"Why are you dumping Milly's cake?" Tom asked.

"Laverne made it."

"Oh for cripes sake!" he said. "Help me get it in the dumpster before someone accidently ingests any of it!"

I laughed despite myself, and helped Tom grab up the clumps of toxic cake and fling them by the handfuls into the dumpster.

"I can't believe you've made me your partner in crime *again*," Tom said as we tossed the last remnants of the public menace into the bin.

"Sorry," I said, and grabbed a towel from my trunk. "I'm afraid I'm a bad influence."

I wiped the cake from Tom's shirt, rubbed my hands on the towel and handed it to him. "It's not so bad. I think your jacket should cover it."

He smiled at me sadly. "See you at the wedding, then."

I walked back to Shabby Maggie and climbed in. Then I suddenly thought of something I wanted to say. I got out and marched up to Tom as he was opening the door to his SUV. I tapped him on the shoulder and swallowed hard.

"Tom, I don't want to be your partner in crime," I said as he turned around to face me.

"I know," he said softly. "You've made that clear."

"No. No I haven't. What I mean, is, I want to be your *partner*, Tom, plain and simple. Will you...would you...ask me again?" I held the blue sapphire ring in my open hand for him to see.

"Really?" he asked.

"Really," I said.

"Right here?" He asked, his sea-green eyes twinkling. "In front of the dumpster flies, the beer bottles and everything?"

I smiled as tears brimmed my eyes. "Yes. Right here. Right now."

He laid the towel down and got on one knee. "Valliant Jolly Fremden, will you marry me?"

I smiled. "Yes, Thomas Foreman. I'll marry you."

Tom slipped the ring on my finger and kissed me hard on the mouth. "I thought you didn't want me," he whispered.

"I've never wanted anything more," I said. "We've been fools."

"Yes," Tom said. "Fools in love."

WITH THE BLUE SAPPHIRE ring back on my finger, the wedding went off without a hitch. The weather was perfect, and the sunset over the Gulf was custom-made for a couple in love. Everyone wore their Sunday best, and when we raised a toast to Milly and Vance, I'd never seen a couple more radiant with happy expectations.

"The deed is done," I whispered in Jorge's ear as I hugged him. "Now we just have to cut the cake. It looks marvelous!"

"Yeah," Jorge said. "Only I didn't know what kind of cake was inside. I took a guess and made carrot."

"Oh," I said. "I'm sure it will be delicious."

Winky came up with Winnie on his arm. He was sporting the worst haircut I'd ever seen.

"Geeze, Winky. Did you fall asleep in a vat of electric shavers?"

"Watch your gator mouth a'fore it gets your chicken butt in trouble," he joked, and stuck his freckled nose in the air proudly. "I'll have you know I donate my head as a Guinea pig for barbers in trainin'. It's my contribution to society."

Goober joined our little circle. "So, what are you gonna do now that pet cremation is off the table?" I asked.

"Off the grill, you mean," Goober said. "I dunno. I may help Winkie and Winnie out. Or maybe become Jorge's secretary. He landed a job as office manager down at the St. Pete station."

"Jorge!" I cried out and patted him on the back. "You didn't say!"

"Yeah, he'll be back in the old division," Tom said. "We'll be partners again."

"Good for you!" Vance said. "But does anyone know who the old drunk broad dressed in black is?" Vance asked.

"My mom," Milly said with a smirk. "Welcome to the family."

Vance stuck a finger in his collar to loosen it as we laughed and patted him on the back.

"Yes, welcome to the family," we all said.

"Er...I guess now would be a good time to cut the cake," Vance said.

"I'd keep an eye on that knife," Winky joked.

"Yes! Cut the cake!" Laverne said, and jumped up and down with enthusiasm.

While Milly and Vance posed for pictures in front of the cake, Tom came and put his arm around me. Laverne stood beside us, her eyes glued to the cake. The wedding pair took the knife and cut into the cake together as everyone cheered. As they fed chunks of golden-orange cake to each other, I heard Laverne gasp.

I looked over at the funny, kooky old sage who'd become my friend. She was crying.

"Geeze, Laverne," I whispered. "Is something wrong?"

"The cake," she said. "It's a wedding miracle!"

WHILE EVERYONE DANCED in the moonlight, Tom took me by the hand. "Let's take a walk," he said.

We strolled along the gentle shore of the Gulf of Mexico, a scene that I knew so well. But tonight it seemed different somehow as I watched the starlight dance in Tom's golden blond hair.

"I want us to be happy together," Tom said. He stopped and picked up a small shell. He studied it for a moment, then flung it back in the water.

"Me, too," I said.

"Why were you so unsure about us?" he asked.

"It wasn't you I ever doubted, Tom. It was me. I was afraid I didn't love you enough. You deserve someone who's completely gaga over you. I'm not the gaga type. I'm more of the...I dunno...process-of-elimination type."

Tom laughed softly and kissed me. "You're also the honest type. I don't want to force you if you're not ready."

"I wonder, Tom. How can you be so sure *I'm* the one? What's so special about me?"

"It's not *you*, per se," he teased.

"Oh. Thanks."

Tom laughed and squeezed my hand. "No. I didn't mean it like that. It's more the way *I* am when I'm around you. All your pain-in-the-butt challenges and questions...they keep me on my toes. When I'm with you, I feel *awake...alive.*"

"Oh."

"You know, despite all your bravado, Val Fremden, you *need* me. Everybody needs someone. I guess what I'm trying to say is, I think my best shot at happiness is with you."

"Cold Cuts says happiness is a choice."

Tom took me in his arms. "She's right. It *is*. I choose *you*."

"But Tom, if I wear this ring, I'll be different."

"What do you mean?"

"I'll be...*un-cursed.*"

"What are you talking about?"

"The ring. It...*changes* me. If I wear it, I won't be klutzy anymore. Or disaster prone. Or have weird things happen to me anymore. You see, this ring – it takes all that away. It makes me...*normal.*"

"Val, that's crazy –"

"Watch," I said. I took the ring off and handed it to Tom.

I took a few steps down the beach. My foot landed on a conch shell. I tripped and fell face-first in the sand. Tom ran up and knelt beside me. He held my hand and patted my back as I hacked out a mouthful of sand and seaweed.

"Are you okay?"

"I will be," I sputtered. "When you put the ring back on me."

Tom fished the ring from his shirt pocket. "Val, are you saying that if you wear this ring, you'll have a normal life?"

"Yes. That's exactly what I'm saying."

"Well then, here goes," he said. Tom stood up, reared back his hand and flung the ring as hard as he could into the ocean.

"Tom! What did you do that for?"

"Because I don't want a normal life, Val. I want the kind of life I have with you."

"But Tom! The –"

"Shhh," Tom said, and shook his head softly. "All the weird stuff is the best part, Val. With you, I know our lives will never be boring."

"But what about the getting married part?" I asked.

Tom knelt beside me and brushed the sand from my face. Then he used a finger to draw a question in the sand.

"Do you love me?" he wrote.

"Yes," I said. "I really do."

He smiled and swept me up in his arms. "Then that's plenty enough for me."

DEAR READER,

Thanks so much for reading Five Oh! I hope you enjoyed the story. Val bit the big one this time. A half a century and still so far to go....

For Val, age is just a number. She's been set back to zero so many times, she's quit counting everything but sheep. So the big five-oh birthday was no big deal. Not compared to Tom's matrimonial advances, anyway. We all know we can't stop time from marching on. But we *can* keep people from marching all over us. In Five Oh, Val hammers out a way to add people to her life without subtracting from her own. Basic math for some. But not for all. How about you?

If you'd like to know when my future novels come out, please subscribe to my newsletter. I won't sell your name or send too many notices to your inbox.

Newletter Link: https://dl.bookfunnel.com/fuw7rbfx21

Thanks again for reading my book! For some, life begins at forty. Others, fifty. I say, life begins today. Make it a good one! ;)

Sincerely,

Margaret Lashley

P.S. If you'd like to check out the next book in the series, Six Tricks, I've included a sample for you in the back of this book. Or click here:

https://www.amazon.com/dp/B07BPMC22T

P.S.S. I live for reviews! The link to leave yours is right here:

https://www.amazon.com/dp/B078BHWQPR#customerReviews

P.S.S.S. (Sounds like Maggie's got a flat!) If you'd like to contact me, you can reach me by:

Website: https://www.margaretlashley.com

Email: contact@margaretlashley.com

Facebook: https://www.facebook.com/valandpalspage/

What's Next for Val?

I hope you enjoyed Five Oh: Fifty is the New F-Word. Click the link below now and leave a review. I read every single one!
https://www.amazon.com/dp/B078BHWQPR#customerReviews
Thank you so much! You rock!
Don't miss another new release! Follow me on Amazon and BookBub and you'll be notified of every new crazy Val adventure.
Follow me on Amazon:
https://www.amazon.com/-/e/B06XKJ3YD8
Follow me on BookBub:
https://www.bookbub.com/search/authors?search=Margaret%20Lashley
Ready for more Val?
Val survived turning fifty, and getting engaged. But Tom's not done with his relationship roulette just yet. What's he up to next?
Enjoy the following excerpt from the next Val Fremden Mystery:
Six Tricks: Doggone Disaster!

Six Tricks Excerpt

Chapter One

"**I**'m too old and set in my ways for this crap," Laverne said. She rolled her big, bulgy eyes and handed me a Tanqueray and tonic. It was in a highball glass she'd filched from the Flamingo Casino decades ago, back in her Vegas-showgirl days.

"Tell me about it," I groused, and took a sip from the glass. The cartoon caricature of a cross-eyed, long-necked pink bird stared back at me. Its expression seemed oddly appropriate. "What are we gonna do?"

"I don't know," Laverne said. "But we better think of something fast. It's driving me crazy!" The old woman pursed her thin lips, then threw back her horsey head and chugged her Dirty Shirley like a merchant marine at last call. She slammed the glass on the counter and said, "Come with me, Val. I got something to show you."

I followed Laverne's shriveled, brown butt cheeks down the hall toward her bedroom. As I watched her two raisin-like buttocks wobble back and forth, I couldn't decide which view of the tall, skinny, seventy-something woman in a gold thong bikini was more disconcerting, the front or the back.

"Get a look at this," Laverne snarled. She threw open her closet door, spun around to face me, and stabbed a red-lacquered fingernail at the source of her disdain. "He's commandeered nearly *half* the lower rack!"

I followed the trajectory of her high-gloss fingertip to a spot about midway down the closet wall. Hanging on the bottom rung of Laverne's huge walk-in closet were about a dozen diminutive men's shirts and pants, along with a sweater and a sport jacket. Together, they were eating away at well over a foot of precious closet space. It was a single woman's worst nightmare. And soon, if Tom had his way, it would be my nightmare, too.

"Geeze!" I said. "That's the most disturbing thing I've seen since Uncle Jack's comb-over!"

Laverne scrunched her red lips into the shape of an inflamed sphincter. "That's not even the worst of it."

"What?" I tore my eyes from the horrific scene. "I mean...how...what?"

"J.D. doesn't like me sunbathing," Laverne complained. "He says it wrinkles my skin. And...you're not going to believe this." Laverne stared into my eyes. Her penciled-on eyebrows formed twin pyramids just below her strawberry-blonde curls. "He *hates my gold thong*, Val!"

Laverne straightened her back and stuck out her pendulous boobs, clothed only in two woefully inadequate triangles of glittery, gold fabric. "J.D. says it's not dignified. Can you believe it? If I wanted to be *dignified*, don't you think I'd have gone and done it by now? I'd have moved into one of those blasted...what 'cha call 'em? *Anal-retentive* communities."

"I believe the term is *deed restricted* communities."

"That's it!" Laverne's angular eyebrows rounded themselves into McDonald's arches. "I don't want to be deed restricted, Val." She pouted as her shoulders slumped. "I love J.D., but it ain't worth it if I have to give up *myself* in the process."

I bit my lip and looked down. I couldn't have said it better myself. But maybe my mom, Glad Goldrich, could have. Glad once told me that no one could stop change. And whether a particular change *itself* was good or bad depended on your perspective. Well, the way I saw it, the changes hurtling toward me and my neighbor Laverne were neither good *nor* bad. They were downright, gut-flopping *terrifying*.

The night of Vance and Milly's wedding, I thought I'd dodged the bullet and put the whole matrimony debate between me and my boyfriend Tom to rest. When he'd flung our cursed engagement ring in the ocean, I'd thought that meant my troubles were over.

Boy, had I been wrong.

Right after he'd tossed the ring, Tom had explained to me that he could live with the way things were...the operative term being *live with*. He'd told me he wanted us to play house – as in, *live together!* Crap on a cracker! The way I saw relationships, marriage was just a ceremony. The *real* work was surviving *cohabitation*. Misery didn't love company. Misery *was* company – if you had no choice in the matter.

The mere thought of coming home to find Tom in my space *every single blasted day for the rest of my life* had set my teeth to gnashing. But if there was one consolation – ironic as it was – it was the fact that *I wasn't alone* in my dilemma. Laverne was trying to bail her way out of the same sinking boat. Mr. J.D. Fellows, Esq., it seemed, had his eye on moving in with *her*.

"You got any ideas how to deal with this catastrophe?" Laverne asked as I stared blankly at the man-infestation slowly taking over her closet.

"Not a dang clue," I muttered.

"Aww, crap," Laverne said, and slammed the closet door shut.

BACK HOME, I TIPSILY eyeballed my *own* bedroom closet. It was half as big as Laverne's. And Tom was twice the size of J.D. Fellows. I didn't like the way the math was adding up....

I heard a light rap on my front door. I closed the closet and padded barefoot down the hall. But before I could answer the door, it opened on its own. Tom strolled in like he owned the place.

"Hi there, cutie!" he said, and gave me one of his irresistible winks.

For the first time, Tom's handsome, blond, sea-green-eyed magic didn't work on me. It had been rendered powerless by what he carried in his left hand.

"What have you got in the duffle bag?" I asked, and eyed them both suspiciously.

"Just a couple of things," he said, and kissed me on the lips.

My heart skipped a beat. But not from his kiss.

Just a couple of things, my behind! Thanks to my earlier pow-wow with Laverne, I knew what this was. It was the first step in Tom's insidious plan to...to...to *what?* Invade my space? Take over my life? Destroy my world as I knew it?

Well, that was the million-dollar question, wasn't it? Only this time, I didn't have a million dollars to lose....

Keep reading! Get your copy of Six Tricks on Amazon:
https://www.amazon.com/dp/B07BPMC22T

About the Author

Like the characters in my novels, I haven't lead a life of wealth or luxury. In fact, as it stands now, I'm set to inherit a half-eaten jar of Cheez Whiz...if my siblings don't beat me to it.

During my illustrious career, I've been a roller-skating waitress, an actuarial assistant, an advertising copywriter, a real estate agent, a house flipper, an organic farmer, and a traveling vagabond/truth seeker. But no matter where I've gone or what I've done, I've always felt like a weirdo.

I've learned a heck of a lot in my life. But getting to know myself has been my greatest journey. Today, I know I'm smart. I'm direct. I'm jaded. I'm hopeful. I'm funny. I'm fierce. I'm a pushover. And I have a laugh that makes strangers come up and want to join in the fun. In other words, I'm a jumble of opposing talents and flaws and emotions. And it's all good.

In some ways, I'm a lot like Val Fremden. My books featuring Val are not autobiographical, but what comes out of her mouth was first formed in my mind, and sometimes the parallels are undeniable. I drink TNTs. I had a car like Shabby Maggie. And I've started my life over four times, driving away with whatever earthly possessions fit in my car. And, perhaps most importantly, I've learned that friends come from unexpected places.